**With love to Eilidh and Aidan, who make
Scotland a better place just by being there. C.S.**

A note on the maps in this book
The maps in this book are for illustrative purposes only and should not be relied on for accuracy.

A note on the pronunciation of Gaelic and Scots words
Every effort has been made to ensure that this information is correct at the time of going to print. Any errors will be corrected upon reprint.

Published in the UK by Scholastic, 2023
1 London Bridge, London, SE1 9BG
Scholastic Ireland, 89E Lagan Road, Dublin Industrial Estate, Glasnevin, Dublin, D11 HP5F

SCHOLASTIC and associated logos are trademarks and/or
registered trademarks of Scholastic Inc.

Text © Chae Strathie, 2023
Illustration for 'The Story of Scotland' © Hazel Dunn, 2023
Illustration for 'City and Country' © Jill Calder, 2023
Illustration for 'Warring Scotland' © Catriona Phillips, 2023
Illustration for 'Haunted Scotland' © Helen Kellock, 2023
Illustration for 'Legendary Scotland' © Lauren Morsley, 2023
Illustration for 'The Culture of Scotland' © Katie Smith, 2023

Cover illustration by Hazel Dunn

Dennis the Menace illustration on p.100 is used by kind permission of DC Thomson & Co Ltd.

The TARDIS image and DOCTOR WHO word mark are registered trade marks belonging to the BBC.

ISBN 978 07023 1626 5

A CIP catalogue record for this book is available from the British Library.

All rights reserved.
This book is sold subject to the condition that it shall not, by way of trade or otherwise, be lent, hired out or otherwise circulated in any form of binding or cover other than that in which it is published. No part of this publication may be reproduced, stored in a retrieval system, or transmitted in any form or by any other means (electronic, mechanical, photocopying, recording or otherwise) without prior written permission of Scholastic Limited.

Printed in China
Paper made from wood grown in sustainable forests and other controlled sources.

1 3 5 7 9 10 8 6 4 2

www.scholastic.co.uk

SCOTLAND

The people
The places • The stories

Chae Strathie

Foreword by
Lorraine Kelly

SCHOLASTIC

CONTENTS

Foreword	8
Introduction	12
The Story of Scotland	14
City and Country	30
Warring Scotland	46

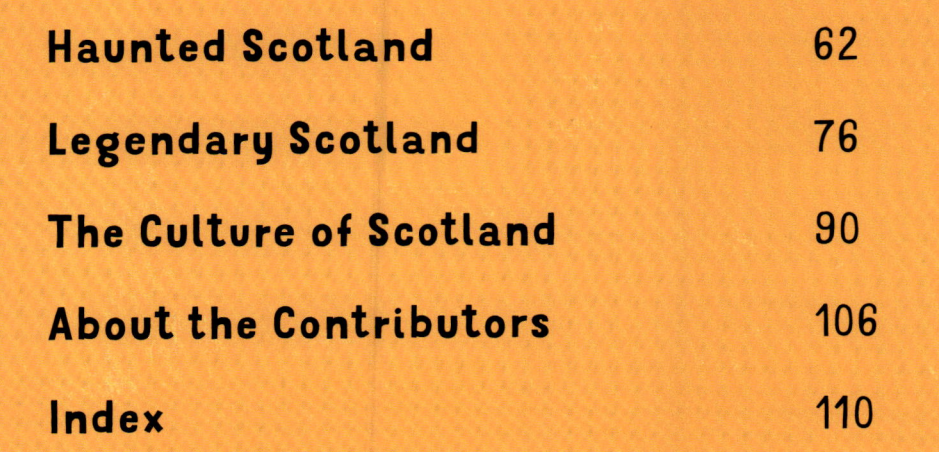

Haunted Scotland	62
Legendary Scotland	76
The Culture of Scotland	90
About the Contributors	106
Index	110

FOREWORD

Lorraine Kelly

Anyone who was born in Scotland is fiercely proud to be Scottish and I am no different.

I've been lucky enough to have travelled all over this beautiful country of mine, meeting some of the most warm-hearted and friendly people and being in constant awe at the superb scenery.

I was born in Glasgow in 1959 and spent the first few years of my life in a "single-end" in the Gorbals, with my mum and dad in one small room, sharing an outside toilet with all the neighbours.

We moved up in the world to Bridgeton in the East End of the city, to a room and kitchen with the unimaginable luxury of an inside loo! When they knocked down our tenement, we were part of the "overspill" shipped out to the new town of East Kilbride.

I joined the local weekly newspaper straight out of school, and in 1984 when I became the Scottish correspondent for breakfast TV station TVam, I filmed in some of the most remote, interesting and unforgettable parts of Scotland.

I witnessed the Up Helly Aa celebrations in Shetland on a freezing January evening, warmed up when flaming torches flew over our heads to set fire to a life-sized replica of a Viking ship.

I began a love affair with Orkney that has me going back every year just to breathe in the air and explore islands like Hoy, Westray and North Ronaldsay.

I've been to Fair Isle and Foula and also discovered the stunning beaches on Harris in the Outer Hebrides. The white sands and clear turquoise water could be straight from a brochure for the Maldives, if it wasn't for the bracing breezes!

I even made it to St Kilda, an archipelago 64 kilometres (40 miles) west of the Outer Hebrides which is haunted by ghosts. You can visit the houses of the inhabits who were evacuated back in the 1930s and really feel as though you are on the edge of the world.

I've seen giant red deer in the Cairngorms, massive sea eagles flying over Mull, watched otters frolicking on the Orkney mainland, dolphins on the crossing to Iona, and the tide roaring in on the Solway Firth.

As you will learn from this brilliant book, Scotland has a rich and vibrant history with some good and noble figures not to mention a few downright villains.

The stories of their lives are fascinating and sometimes almost unbelievable.

Going right back in time, I think most of us have seen *Braveheart* on the big screen with Mel Gibson playing the hero William Wallace.

Although Mel took a few liberties with the plot, what he did get absolutely right was the passion, charisma and sheer cheek (we did actually see a few bare bums!) of the Scottish clans who supported "The Wallace".

Mary Queen of Scots is still a woman who continues to fascinate authors and film makers; our national bard Robert Burns is as relevant today as ever he was, and all over the world people sing his "Auld Lang Syne" at Hogmanay.

Our whisky is often copied but never equalled, and we have our very own monster who shyly lives at the bottom of Loch Ness.

Scottish beef, lamb, cheese, fish and seafood are the best in the world and tartan never goes out of fashion.

But it's the people who make Scotland and there's no better welcome than a wee Glasgow wumman chatting with you at the bus stop, an Edinburgh taxi driver telling you all about the famous festival or a Highland hotelier proudly showing you round his little piece of heaven.

Enjoy reading this wonderful book and discovering more about Scotland.

INTRODUCTION

Do you think you know everything there is to know about Scotland?

Is your brain BURSTING with fascinating facts about the country, its people and its history?

Well, let's put that to the test with our super-hard multiple-choice quiz.

Every single person in Scotland wears:

A. Massive kilts – even in bed

B. Onesies woven from Highland cow hair

C. Just jeans and hoodies and stuff

A haggis is:

A. A funny little animal that roams the mountains until it is caught for tea

B. A type of disgusting brown fruit that grows on haggis trees, which can be found on the shores of Loch Lomond

C. A delicious dish made of meat (or veggie stuff), oats and spices that is traditionally eaten on Burns Night (25 January)

The sound of bagpipes is commonly met with:
....

A. Shrieks of pain and loud wailing

B. The clatter of feet running away

C. Joyful cries of "YEEEE-OOCH!", enthusiastic clapping and loud stomping

How did you do? Are you good enough to be immediately crowned king or queen of Scotland, or should you never show your face north of Hadrian's Wall again?

If you answered mostly Cs, you are officially a Scottishologist, and can call yourself Professor Insert-your-name-here. If you answered mostly As or Bs, you really need a crash course in all things Scottish before you even THINK about taking a sip of Irn-Bru again. Luckily, this book has the answers to the above questions and much, much more, so you can become a TOTAL EXPERT!

So read on…

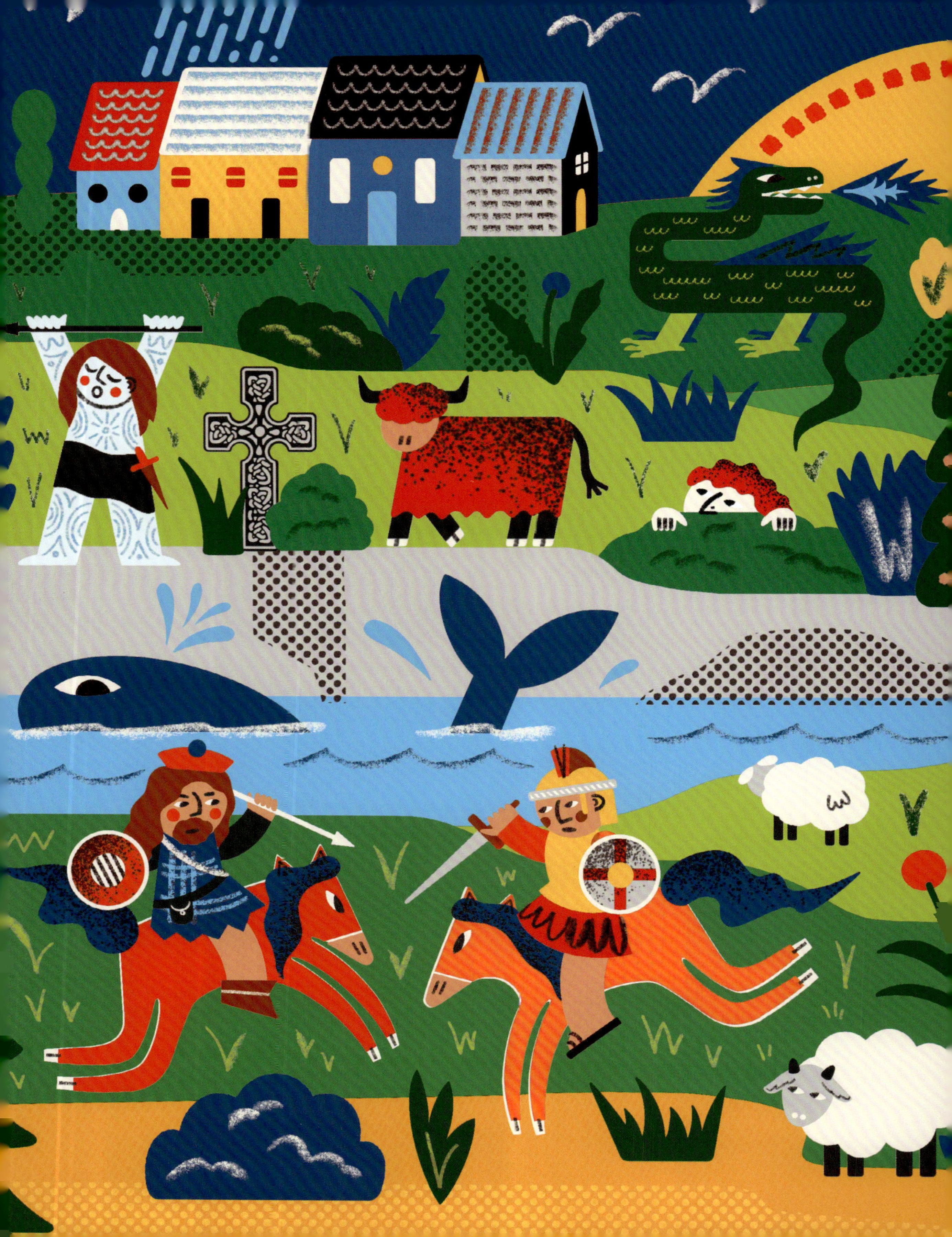

THE STORY OF SCOTLAND

SCOTLAND

Population – **5.5 million**

Edinburgh is the capital city of Scotland.

There are **32 council areas** in Scotland.

Isle of Skye dinosaur tracks

Ben Nevis

Iona

Antonine Wall

The westernmost point on the mainland of Great Britain is **Corrachadh Mòr, Highland.**

CANADA 3,115 km (1,935 miles)

IRELAND 23 km (14 miles)

USA 4,119 km (2,560 miles)

ORKNEY 16 km (10 miles)

Skara Brae

SHETLAND 210 km (130 miles)

NORWAY 303 km (188 miles)

JOHN O'GROATS

The northernmost point on the mainland of Great Britain is **Dunnet Head, Caithness.**

The biggest region by area is **Highland** at 25,657 sq km, and the smallest is **Dundee City** at 59 sq km.

Forth Bridge

Biggar

The biggest region by population is **Glasgow City**, which has 626,410 people, and the smallest is **Orkney** with 22,190.

Southern Uplands

THE STORY OF SCOTLAND

Scotland is old. Really old.

We're talking even older than that box of porridge at the back of the cupboard that went out of date before you were even born.

Scotland's age depends on whether you're talking about the rocks or the people. On the geological front, you'd have to travel back three billion years to see the earliest rocks being formed. Don't forget to pack a cheese sandwich for the journey – that's a long time ago!

The oldest rocks in Scotland are the **Lewisian gneisses**, which are found in the Northwest Highlands and across to the islands of the Outer Hebrides. Actually, they are not only the oldest rocks in Scotland – they are among the oldest rocks in Europe!

And get this for a mind-melting Scottish rock fact: the hill Roineabhal on the island of Harris is made of ancient rocks called anorthosite, which are similar in composition to rocks found in the mountains of the Moon. So Scotland really is out of this world!

Enough of the stony stuff for now – what about the people? They haven't been here for quite as long. The earliest evidence of humans in Scotland dates from around 14,000 years ago. Back in 2005, archaeologists discovered more than 5,000 flint objects dated to around 12,000 BC in a field near the town of Biggar in South Lanarkshire. The tools are very similar to ones from the same period found in Germany and Denmark, so experts think it's possible the people who used them walked over the land that once connected Britain to the European continent. At least that saved them the cost of an aeroplane ticket!

About 1,000 years after that, an ice age froze Scotland and made it more or less uninhabitable for around 1,000 years – even with a woolly hat and nice thick socks. But when everything melted, humans headed back and we've been here ever since.

GEOLOGY

The story of Scotland's landscape involves changes that took place over billions of years, and are still happening today – though thankfully with fewer volcanoes.

Ask people from around the globe to name one thing that they associate with Scotland's natural beauty and almost all of them will say "hills and mountains". Huge mountains over 914 metres (3,000 feet) are known as **Munros**, hills between 762 to 914 m (2,500–3,000 ft) are called **Corbetts**, those between 607 to 762 m (2,000–2500 ft) are called **Grahams** and hills in the Scottish Lowlands over 607 m (2,000 ft) are called **Donalds**.

The biggest mountain in Britain, **Ben Nevis**, is in Scotland. Its summit is 1,345 m (4,413 ft) above sea level, and it was once an enormous volcano that collapsed in on itself. Although that might be the most impressive mountain in terms of height, there are plenty more that are just as majestic in other ways. They were formed from incredible forces that moved continents, made entire oceans disappear and caused rocks to erupt from the ground and reach for the sky.

One of the most important events in the history of Scotland's geology was called the **Caledonian Orogeny**. It involved parts of what would become Scotland, North America, England,

Wales and Ireland smashing into each other – though when we say "smash" it happened over 150 million years, so it wasn't exactly quick. It also happened 500 million years ago, so you probably didn't notice it.

The Iapetus Ocean that existed at the time was closed up by the continents coming together. Rocks were crushed and forced upwards to form much of the Highlands, as well as the Southern Uplands, a range of hills that stretches from west to east across the bottom of Scotland. Throw in a few volcanoes and ice ages, when glaciers over a kilometre (half a mile) thick carved their way across the land, and you can see why Scotland's landscape looks so breathtakingly wild, magnificent and varied.

And it isn't over yet! The land is still being changed by river and coastal erosion – so who knows what Scotland will look like a few hundred million years from now? You'll have to pop down to your local time machine shop to find out.

EARLY SCOTLAND

Let's leave the rocks behind and go back to visit those early people we mentioned. We can't call them Scots yet, because Scotland as a nation didn't exist when they were doing all their hunting and gathering 14,000 years ago.

After the ice had thawed, people returned to Scotland and started settling over the next few thousand years. To begin with, they would have moved around, following the animals they hunted to survive. Wild horses and reindeer were among the creatures they ate, and they used the animals' bodies to make everything from clothing and blankets to shelters and tools. Early humans would even have shared the land with bears, wolves and lynxes, which would have made the walk to school interesting (not that they had schools back then). Having said that, "A bear ate my homework!" is an excellent excuse.

Around 4000 BC, in the **Neolithic period**, people began coming together and living in settlements as they learned how to cultivate the land to grow crops. They also learned how to farm animals, so they didn't have to keep chasing them around with spears. This was great for the people, but probably less popular among cows, sheep and pigs.

It was during this prehistoric time that the people who settled in the Orkney Islands off the north coast of Scotland built some of the most stunning monuments and tombs in the world.

Maeshowe, which was built around 5,000 years ago, is a tomb that was carefully designed so that the sun shines right down the entrance passageway, flooding the main chamber with light on the winter solstice, which is the shortest day of the year.

Skara Brae, also on Orkney, is a small village dating back to 3200 BC. The houses were connected by covered passages, which meant residents could travel from home to home without stepping outside, keeping them out of the wild Orkney weather. They even had stone beds and seats, which were advanced for the time but, let's face it, probably won't make a comeback any time soon.

The arrival of the Bronze Age around 4,500 years ago, followed by the Iron Age, meant people could make better tools and weapons and more elaborate jewellery. From then, it was only a matter of time before everyone had a smartphone and a games console.

ROMAN VISITORS

It can be nice when people come to visit. Like when your friends come over for a mammoth gaming session. But not all visitors are that welcome. Especially if they want to take over and poke you with sharp things.

That's exactly what the Romans tried to do in Scotland – or **Caledonia**, as they called it – back in the day. The Romans first invaded Britain in 55 BC, after landing at Kent in the south of England, although they didn't really properly get going until AD 43. It took another thirty years before they made it to Scotland, which just shows how slow the buses were back then.

Over the next seven years, during the AD 70s, the Caledonian tribes made a stand against Roman general Julius Agricola, who attacked them by both land and sea. His army built forts across the centre of the land to keep the wild northern Celtic warriors at bay. The Roman army hung around for a while, before slowly leaving to take on other "poking people with sharp things" jobs elsewhere in the empire. They came back again for a second invasion and built the **Antonine Wall** (named after emperor Antoninus Pius) around AD 142. But again, they didn't stick around for terribly long and, shortly after old Antonius died in AD 161, the Antonine Wall was abandoned and the troops headed south to Hadrian's Wall. Despite various campaigns and invasions after that, the Romans never conquered Scotland and they left Britain for good in the year 410.

LANGUAGE

If you're not Scottish and you meet a Scottish person who's very excited and speaking super-fast, you might wish they had subtitles. We can use words and phrases you've probably never heard of – but we're not making them up, honest! There's more about these words and phrases in a moment, but for now let's focus on a language that everyone associates with Scotland: **Gaelic**.

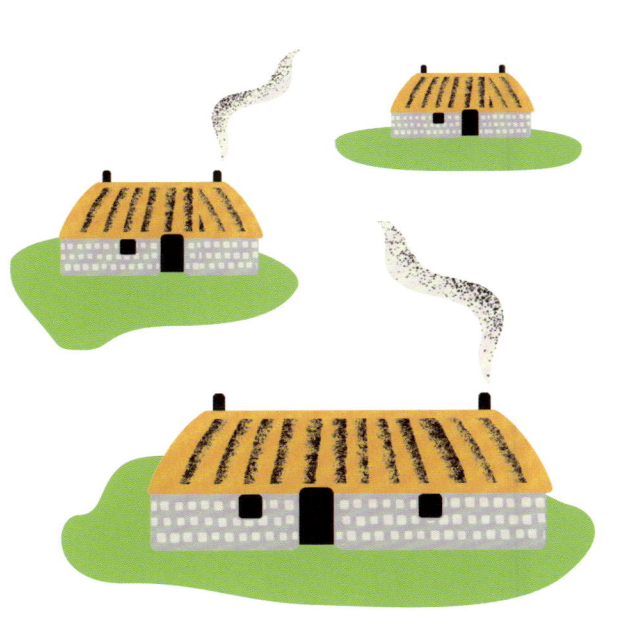

Gaelic didn't originate in Scotland. It is thought that it was brought there from Ireland in the sixth century. But when it did arrive, it quickly became fashionable, spreading across the country from west to east and north to south.

In the late eighteenth century, the notorious **Highland Clearances** got underway. During the clearances, thousands of people were forced off the land and out of their homes in the Highlands and Outer Hebrides by rich landowners. This had a massive impact on Gaelic as communities were broken up and many thousands of people emigrated to North America and elsewhere in the world, never to return.

Although it's not used as widely as it once was, Gaelic is still spoken today by around 60,000 Scots. Just in case you bump into a Gaelic speaker, here's a quick lesson.

GAELIC	PRONUNCIATION	ENGLISH
Madainn mhath	(mateen va)	Good morning
Ciamar a tha thu	(kimmer uh ha oo)	How are you?
Tapadh leibh	(tapa leev)	Thank you
Tha mi duilich	(ha mi doolich)	I'm sorry

So, that's you sorted. You can chat with ease to a Gael, and you won't be havering! Sorry, you don't know what "havering" means? That's because it's a different kind of word – not Gaelic, but **Scots**.

Scots has been spoken in Scotland for centuries, originating around 1,400 years ago. It's one of three native languages spoken in Scotland today, along with English and Gaelic. It's a rich, interesting language, full of wonderful words, and an important part of Scotland's culture.

Here are a few sensational Scots words to get your tongue around.

SCOTS	ENGLISH
Bahookie	Bottom
Blether	A lively chat/someone who talks a lot
Braw	Good/lovely
Coorie	Snuggle
Dook	Dip, dunk or go in water
Fankle	Muddle/tangle
Haver	Talk nonsense
Peelie-wallie	Pale
Shoogle	Shake/wobble
Wheesht	Be quiet

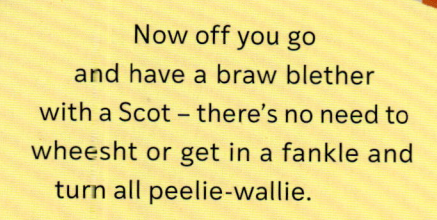

Now off you go and have a braw blether with a Scot – there's no need to wheesht or get in a fankle and turn all peelie-wallie.

THE PICTS

The Picts are probably the best known of the old Scottish groups that were around long ago.

They lived in what is now northern and eastern Scotland, north of the **Firth of Forth**, and were first mentioned by those pesky Romans in around AD 300. The Latin word the Romans used was Picti, which means "painted".

One explanation for this is that the Picts were fond of tattooing themselves. They must have looked pretty strange and fearsome. If your mum or dad has tattoos, you can officially start calling them a Pict, just to confuse them, which is always fun.

The Pictish kingdom is often called Pictland nowadays. Hardly any Pictish writing has survived, but we can get a glimpse into the lives of the Picts through the objects that archaeologists have unearthed, and through the writings of other cultures who mention them. They also carved strange and beautiful designs on lumps of rock, known as **Pictish stones**.

The Picts made up the largest kingdom in Scotland in the Middle Ages, before disappearing from history as they joined with other groups to create the Kingdom of Alba, which would eventually become modern Scotland.

While they may not be around now as a distinct group, us Scots have our Pictish ancestors to thank for the existence of our country. One of the most decisive moments in Pictish – and Scottish – history was the **Battle of Dun Nechtain** on Saturday 2 March, AD 685.

Since AD 653, many groups of people in Scotland, including the Picts, had been ruled by **King Oswiu** from Northumbria in the north of England. When he died in 672, the Picts rose against his successor, Drust. But then a new king of Northumbria, Ecgfrith, rose to power and he took revenge on the Picts, slaughtering thousands of them at a battle near the town of Grangemouth. A few years later, however, it was the Picts' turn to claim victory. Ecgfrith, tried to defeat a Pictish army ruled by **King Bridei Mac Bili** so he could continue to control them.

It didn't quite go according to plan. The battle was a disaster for silly Ecgfrith, who ignored his pals' advice not to do it. His army was destroyed and he was killed, which was very inconvenient for him. That ended the attempts to rule the Picts, and Pictland – and therefore Scotland – continued. Thanks Picts!

WOULD YOU BELIEVE IT?

Although most people accept that **Ben Nevis** is Scotland's tallest mountain at 1,345 m (4,413 ft), some disagree. There is one peak that's 550 m (1,800 ft) higher than Ben Nevis. It's called **Rosemary Bank** and you've probably never heard of it … because it's underwater. It's a massive extinct volcano under the sea to the north-west of the Outer Hebrides. So, if you wanted to climb it, you'd need scuba-diving gear. Rosemary Bank was created by a volcanic eruption around 50 million years ago. If other "seamounts" (underwater peaks formed by volcanic activity) were regarded as mountains, Mount Everest wouldn't be the world's tallest – it would be Mauna Kea, one of the islands that makes up Hawaii. This volcano has a peak of 4,200 m (13,000 ft) above sea level, with the total height of the mountain reaching over 10,200 m (33,500 ft)!

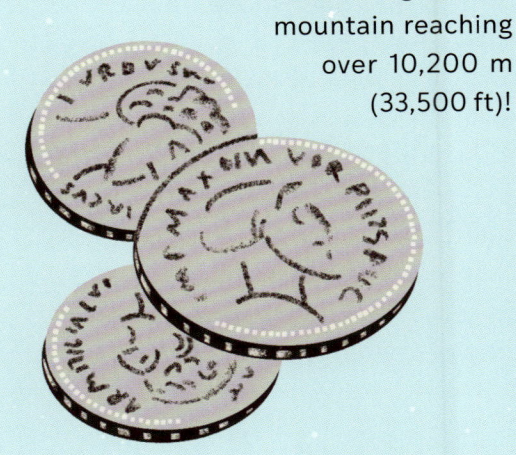

Do you like the idea of finding buried treasure? Silly question – who doesn't love that idea? If you happened to be digging around a hill called **Traprain Law** in East Lothian back in 1919, you might have come across something very exciting. That was when archaeologists discovered a stunning hoard of Roman silver. Buried in the fifth century AD, it's the largest known silver hoard from outside the Roman Empire. It's possible the Romans gave the glittery stuff as a bribe to a native chief to persuade him not to attack south of Hadrian's Wall, which was built across the north of England from AD 122 to guard the wild northern frontier of the Roman Empire.

In the north-east of Scotland, the type of Scots language that is spoken is known as **Doric**. One of the things you'd notice straight away is that the letter "f" is used instead of "h" and "wh" in certain words. That means "how" is pronounced "foo", "what" is "fit". "where" is "far" and "when" is "fan"! The phrase "Foos yer doos?" literally means "How are your pigeons?", but if someone asks you that, don't panic. They just mean "How are you doing?" – you don't have to pretend you have feathered friends.

Caledonia was the name used by the Romans to describe the area that is now much of Scotland. It came from the name of a tribe, the Caledones, whose name can be translated as "possessing hard feet". Luckily for those early Scots, it didn't mean they had problems with their toes, it meant they had endurance and were strong and firm.

In 6200 BC the east coast of Scotland was hit by a 25-m (80-ft) tsunami. The wave was caused by a massive underwater landslide off the coast of Norway. For anyone who lived in the areas affected, it must have been terrifying and catastrophic – any settlements would have been washed away. There had once been a land bridge, now known as Doggerland, that connected Britain to Denmark and the Netherlands. Rising sea levels had slowly covered most of it, making it impossible to get to Amsterdam on roller skates. Some scientists think the tsunami may have submerged the remaining land, Dogger Island, while others believe it survived and people continued to live on it for centuries after that.

3 billion years ago
Scotland's oldest rocks laid down

541 million years ago
Scotland starts its journey north from the South Pole region

201–145 million years ago
Dinosaurs roam Scotland

145–66 million years ago
Much of Scotland is covered by a shallow, warm sea

10,000 BC
Hunter-gatherer societies travel the land in search of food

4000–2500 BC
Neolithic Period

3200 BC
Skara Brae on Orkney built

2800 BC
Maeshowe on Orkney built

2500–500 BC
Bronze Age

500 BC–AD 400
Iron Age

142
The Romans build the **Antonine Wall**

500–1500
Medieval period

563
Saint Columba arrives on Iona, bringing Christianity

1603
The Union of the Crowns brings the monarchy of Scotland and England together

1707
The Act of Union: United Kingdom created as Scotland and England join politically

1712
First Clyde shipyards opened

1750
Highland Clearances begin

1890
Forth Bridge opened

1969
Oil is found in the North Sea

1999
Scottish Parliament established

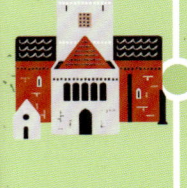

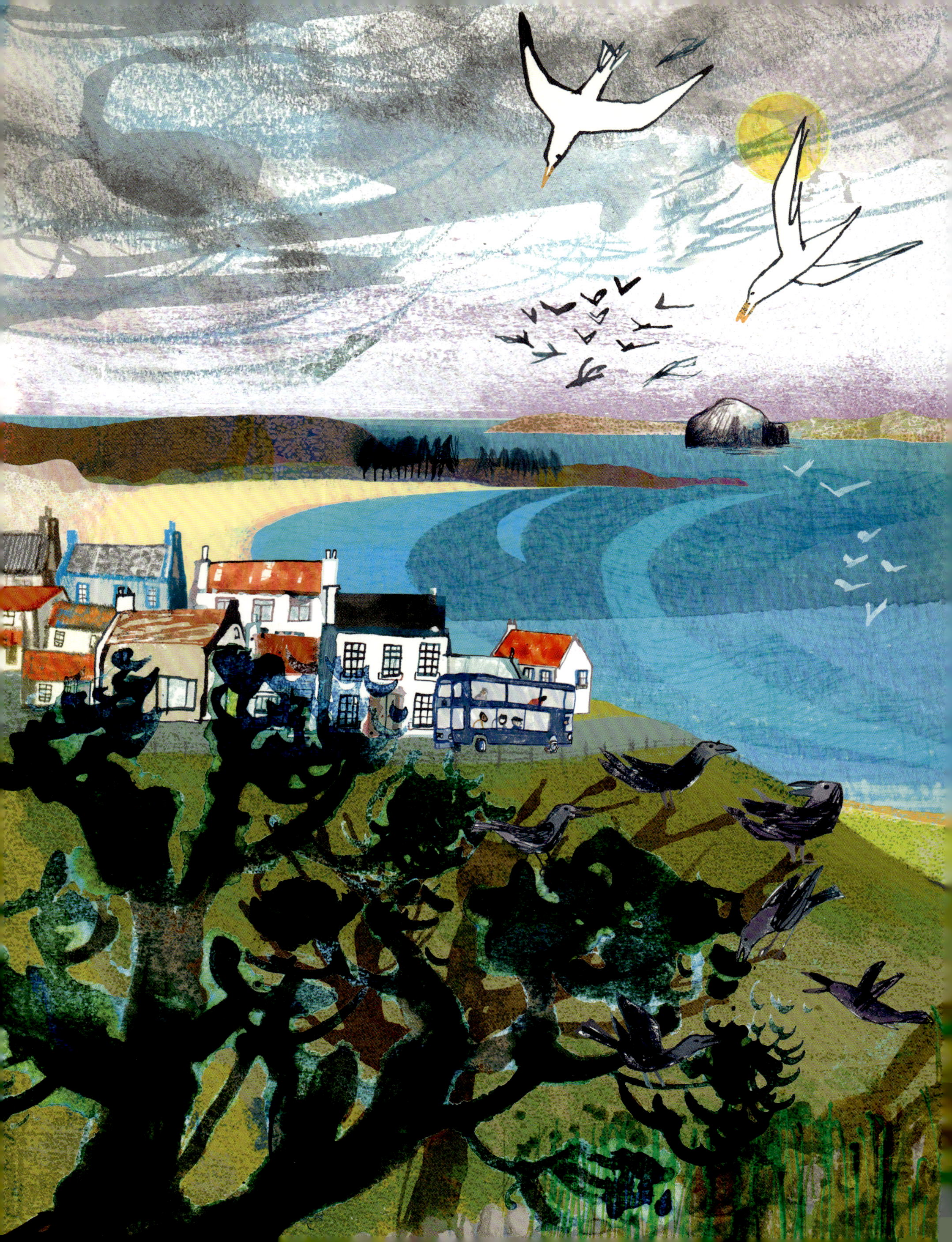

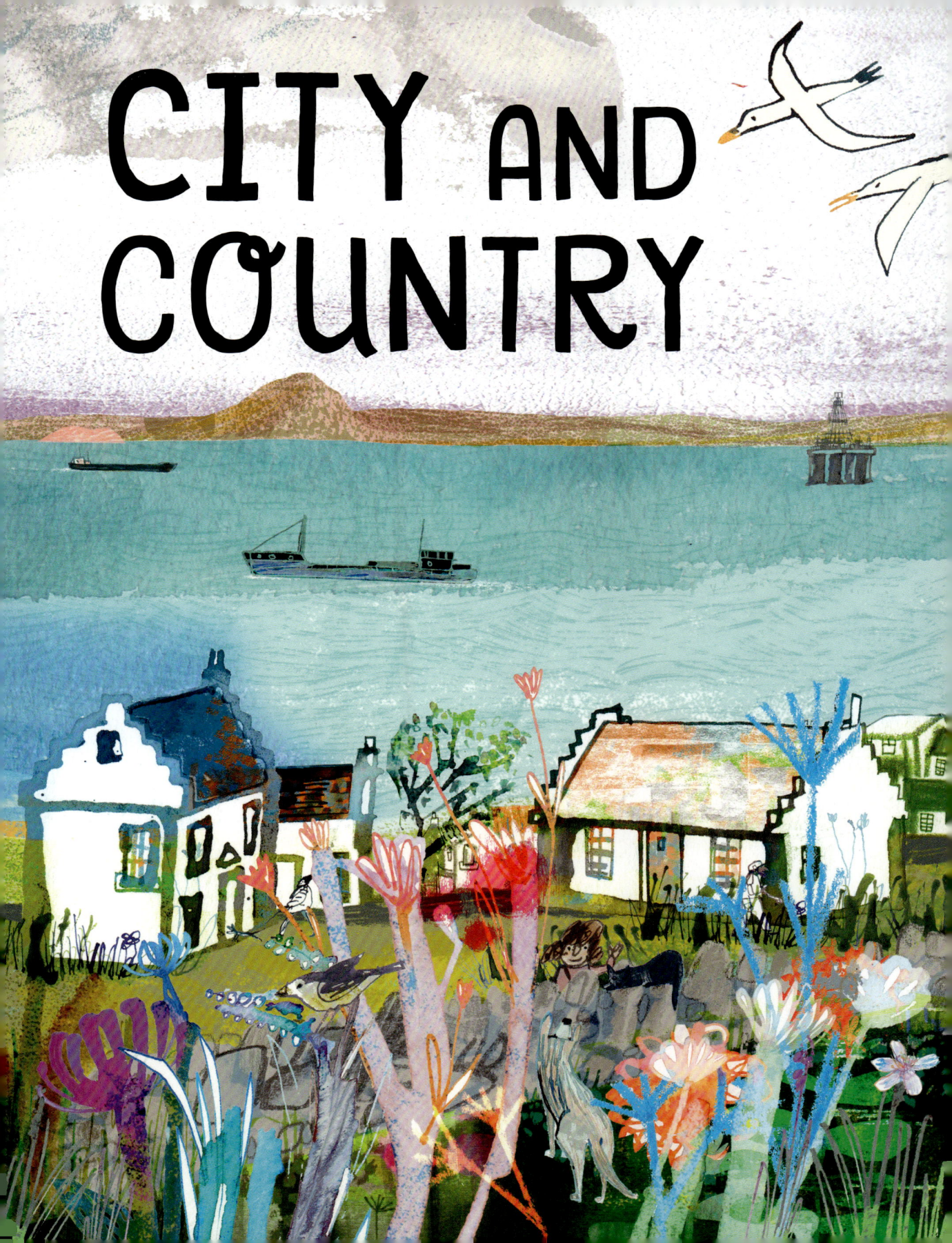

CITY AND COUNTRY

SHETLAND.

210 km
(130 miles)

Aberdeen

ORKNEY.

16 km
(10 miles)

Inverness

Loch Ness

Loch Morar

Outer Hebrides

Skye

Wreck of SS Politician

ROCKALL.

Glenfinnan Viaduct
The Kelpies
River Tay
Dundee
Perth
Secret Bunker
Inchgarvie Island
Central Belt
Edinburgh
Islay
Glasgow
Stirling
New Lanark

CITY AND COUNTRY

Do you like the countryside? Do you enjoy hugging trees and sniffing flowers? Or are you more of a city kid? Do you love the hustle and bustle of busy streets, and the sight of skyscrapers reaching for the clouds? Luckily, in Scotland, there are great things to be discovered in the wilderness and in the city.

The most recent population figures show there are more than 5.4 million people living in Scotland. Most of those Scots dwell in towns and cities in an area known as the Central Belt, which sounds like something you'd wear to keep your breeks (trousers) up. It sits between the Highlands in the north and the Southern Uplands in the south, and takes in Edinburgh and Glasgow. Outside the Central Belt there are some smaller cities, lots of towns and loads of lovely villages dotted around the coastlines, hills, mountains and lochs.

In total, there are seven Scottish cities – Glasgow, Edinburgh, Dundee, Aberdeen, Inverness, Perth and Stirling. Glasgow is the largest, with 1.2 million people living in the Greater Glasgow area, but even that is pretty small compared to the big cities down south. London has a population of around 9 million, for example – nearly double that of the whole of Scotland!

But whether you prefer the vibrant excitement of Scotland's cities or the peace and quiet of the great outdoors, there's something for everyone.

EDINBURGH VS GLASGOW

You know at school if there's someone you quite like, but they also annoy you a bit because they think they're great (although they think you think you're great, too)? That's a bit like Edinburgh and Glasgow.

For as long as people can remember, there's been a rivalry between Scotland's two biggest cities. Glasgow folk reckon Edinburgh folk are a bit stuck up, while Edinburgh people think Glasgow people are rather full of themselves.

The truth is both cities are amazing places full of fabulous people. There are way too many brilliant things about both cities to fit in here, but here are just a few:

Edinburgh is home to festivals that are known the world over. The most famous events happen every summer and include the Edinburgh International Festival, the Edinburgh Fringe Festival (which has nothing to do with hair) and the Edinburgh International Book Festival. The Fringe is the biggest arts festival in the world, sometimes selling more than 3 million tickets for around 50,000 performances of comedy, music, theatre and more.

Aside from the world-famous **Edinburgh Castle**, which has seen much in the way of sieges, battles and intrigue over its 900-year history, the capital also boasts the Scottish Parliament, established in 1999 and the **Palace of Holyroodhouse**, which is the official residence of the monarchy in Scotland. "Rood" is an old word for a crucifix or cross, and the name for Holyroodhouse may have come from a vision of Jesus's cross that King David I was said to have seen, nearly 900 years ago.

Glasgow has just as many wonderful and interesting things as Edinburgh, although it feels quite different. Even though its name means 'green space' in Gaelic, it was a great industrial city, known around the globe for its shipbuilding. It's thought that around 25,000 naval, merchant and passenger ships have been built on the **River Clyde**, which runs through the city, and the largest crane in the world was constructed in Glasgow in 1911.

Nowadays, most of the shipyards are no longer in operation, but the city thrives as a centre of music, art, food, culture and business. It has the third-oldest underground train system in the world, founded in 1896. Because the train carriages are a bright orange colour, it is known locally as "The Clockwork Orange". As a tribute to how lovely Glasgow folk are, it recently topped a poll of the friendliest cities in the world, so do pop along and say hello!

LANDMARKS

There's no shortage of eye-catching buildings, jaw-dropping constructions and mind-blowing monuments all over Scotland.

Leaving aside Edinburgh Castle, probably the next most famous landmark in Scotland is the **Forth Bridge**. This world-famous bridge opened in 1890, and 53,000 tonnes of steel and 6.5 million rivets were used to build it. At one point, more than 4,000 men were employed in its construction. It was dangerous work – sadly at least 73 lives were lost while it was being built.

There's a saying in Scotland that a long task is "like painting the Forth Rail Bridge", as when you get to the end you have to start all over again because it's taken so long to finish. You can see why – the total painted area of the bridge is 230,000 square metres (2,475,700 square feet), which takes 240,000 litres of paint. You'd have a pretty sore arm after painting that!

A more recent landmark is the **Kelpies**. Inspired by mythical water spirits, they are two 30-m- (100-ft-) high stainless steel horse-head sculptures built next to the Forth and Clyde Canal near Falkirk in 2013. Each head has 900 stainless steel scales and weighs 300 tonnes. It's NEIGH wonder they're the MANE attraction in the area (sorry).

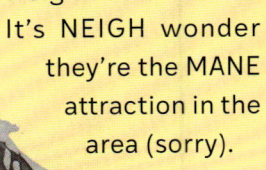

Further north you'll find the **Glenfinnan Viaduct**. If you're a fan of the Harry Potter films, you'll know it well. It's made up of twenty-one enormous arches that curve around the valley past the waters of Loch Shiel. In summer, you can even hop on a steam train to enjoy the same view Harry himself had on his trip to Hogwarts, when the viaduct starred in the movies!

Head east and you'll find a landmark that's been all the way to the South Pole (well, nearly). It's the ship **RRS Discovery**, which took two legendary explorers – **Captain Robert Falcon Scott and Ernest Shackleton** – on their first expedition to Antarctica between 1901 and 1904. It's now moored on the River Tay in Dundee – which is known as the City of Discovery as a result. Unlike most other ships, there are no portholes as they would have weakened the boat's sides under the pressure of the Antarctic ice. Instead, brass vents in the deck provided light and ventilation below. They were easy to walk into, and soon renamed "ankle bashers".

LOCHS

If you don't come from Scotland, here's a wee word of advice – whatever you do, never call an inland body of water a "lake"! It will make Scottish folk turn purple. The correct word is, of course, "loch". It sounds a bit like "lock" but to say the "ch" part properly, you have to do it right at the back of your throat, like you're gargling a handful of gravel. Not everyone can manage it, however, and visitors often just end up saying lock.

There are more than 30,000 freshwater lochs in Scotland. We've got lochs coming out of our ears up here (not literally, of course, as that would be really annoying and make our hats damp).

Which loch rules though? Well, that depends how you want to measure it. **Loch Lomond** has the largest surface area at 71 sq km (27 sq miles), **Loch Morar** is the deepest loch at 310 m (1,017 ft), and **Loch Ness** is the largest loch by volume with more water than all English and Welsh lakes put together (7,452 million cubic metres or 263 billion cubic feet)!

Loch Ness is undoubtedly the most famous around the world, mainly because of a certain monster. But it's not the only loch that has something mysterious lurking in its depths.

Loch Morar is home to **Morag**. Some say she's half human, half fish and heralds a death, while more recent sightings suggest she's a sea monster with humps and a long neck, similar to the **Loch Ness monster.**

Not all lochs are natural. The Nor' Loch was created in the centre of Edinburgh in 1460 to help defend the castle and the city. It was drained in the early eighteenth century and the area it once covered is now a park called Princes Street Gardens.

38

Earlier we said you'd be in big trouble if you called a loch a lake, but there's one place where that's not the case: the Lake of Menteith, near Stirling. Until the nineteenth century, it was known as the Loch of Menteith. No one is entirely certain why it changed names, although it may have been down to a mistake on an early map. It's a bit of a mystery!

ISLANDS

Just like lochs, mountains and castles, Scotland has more islands than we know what to do with. You want an island? Take one – we've got loads!

There are more than **900 islands** off the coast of Scotland, mainly found to the north and west of the country. The poor east coast is pretty much an island-free zone. The biggest island by area and population is, slightly confusingly, called two different things – **Lewis and Harris**. This may sound like two separate islands, but the Isle of Lewis and the Isle of Harris are two parts of one island, separated by mountains.

Lewis and Harris is the main island of the Outer Hebrides, which is the last place in Britain where Gaelic is still spoken on a daily basis by the majority of the population. As well as the Outer Hebrides, there are the Inner Hebrides. The largest island is Skye, while Islay (pronounced "eye-lah") is the most southerly. In the capital, Bowmore, you'll find **Kilarrow Parish Church**, called the Round Church locally. Built in 1767, it's said that it was made completely round to prevent the Devil hiding in any corners!

The island next to Islay is Jura, where red deer outnumber people by twenty-five to one!

Lewis and Harris

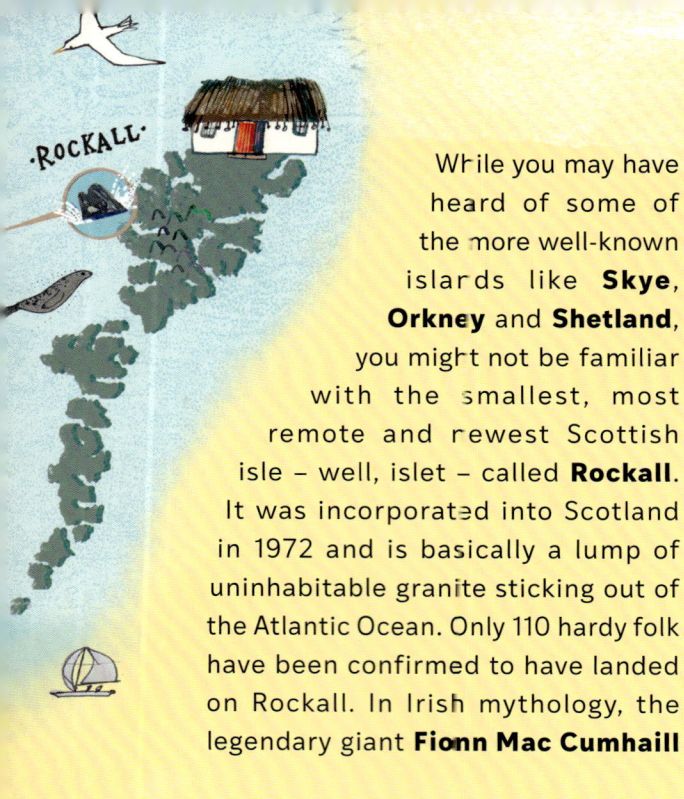

While you may have heard of some of the more well-known islands like **Skye**, **Orkney** and **Shetland**, you might not be familiar with the smallest, most remote and newest Scottish isle – well, islet – called **Rockall**. It was incorporated into Scotland in 1972 and is basically a lump of uninhabitable granite sticking out of the Atlantic Ocean. Only 110 hardy folk have been confirmed to have landed on Rockall. In Irish mythology, the legendary giant **Fionn Mac Cumhaill** (Finn McCool) grabbed a chunk of Ireland to chuck at a Scottish enemy. He missed, and a pebble landed in the sea, forming Rockall. Who knows if that's really true? (Actually, we do. It's not.)

FLORA AND FAUNA

While everyone knows that herds of wild haggises can be spotted roaming in secluded glens, there are lots of other beautiful animals (real ones) that are native to Scotland.

Some have been hunted to extinction or died out. Far back in time, you would have come across woolly rhinos, mammoths and polar bears. More recently, brown bears, elk, wild boar and lynxes roamed free, and official records suggest the last known wolf was shot in **Perthshire** in 1680 (though reports of wolves in Scotland continued into the eighteenth century). Beavers have recently been reintroduced into the wild, while some people want wolves to be brought back in a few remote areas. The idea of bringing wolves back to the Scottish Highlands was first proposed in the late 1960s, but it has become more popular in recent years. Some people are worried it may be dangerous, while others say it will be good for the land as wolves will stop deer damaging woodland saplings. For now, there are no plans to see the hairy howling creatures in a glen any time soon.

Despite some animals dying out, there are plenty of fascinating creatures that can still be discovered – if you're lucky. **Hairy Highland coos** (cows) and red deer are fairly simple to spot.

Slightly harder are majestic golden eagles and sweet red squirrels. But if you really want to earn your "I Spy" points, keep your eyes peeled for the Scottish wildcat or the pine marten.

There are thought to only be around 100–300 wildcats left, as their numbers have dwindled, due to their natural habitats being lost. Another threat to wildcats is hybridization – this is when wildcats breed with pet cats. Their offspring have fewer wildcat features, and more domestic cat features, meaning wildcat features might eventually be lost for ever.

Pine martens are part of the weasel family and can be easily recognized by their cute wee faces and long bodies, although you're very unlikely to ever see one given that there are only around 3,700 left. They sometimes make their homes in birds' nests, so if you ever spot a long, thin, furry pigeon, it might actually be a pine marten.

On the flora front, Scotland's national flower is, of course, the **thistle**. The Roman writer Pliny the Elder thought thistles could make hair return to bald heads! So, if your dad's a bit thin on top, now you know what to get him for his birthday. Why is it held in such high regard in Scotland? Apparently back in the mists of time some sleeping Scots warriors were woken when a Norse soldier who was about to attack them with his comrades stepped on a thistle and yelled out in pain!

SCOTLAND'S WEATHER

There's a saying about places with changeable weather having "four seasons in one day". Well, in Scotland you can have four seasons in one minute. Or at least it feels like that sometimes.

Should you leave the house with a brolly, sunglasses, a scarf or shorts? In Scotland, the answer is often 'all of the above'. And you should probably throw in some skis as well. In July.

Scotland often gets a bad rep as a country where it rains constantly and is freezing cold, but actually the climate is pretty moderate, f unpredictable. Spring temperatures can hit a fairly mild 13 °C (55 °F), and summer heatwaves aren't out of the question. Scotland's high latitude means summer days are longer, and twilight (or "gloaming" if you're in Scotland) can be especially lingering and lovely. Incredibly, Lerwick in Shetland has about four hours more daylight in the middle of summer than London!

Winter can be chilly – but that's sort of to be expected. And if snowboarding and sledging are your bag, the mountains and hills get around a hundred days of the white stuff on average.

So don't worry about the weather. Just come prepared for all types of it at once.

WOULD YOU BELIEVE IT?

On 5 February 1941, a ship called the **SS Politician** ran aground on the island of Eriskay. It was laden with 260,000 bottles of whisky, and when the locals learned from the crew what the ship was carrying, they valiantly set off to rescue it! Wartime rationing meant whisky supplies on the islands had run low, so the islanders helped themselves to around 24,000 bottles. The local customs officer and police tried to find the missing bottles, but most were hidden (or drunk) to avoid confiscation. The hull of the ship was blown up to stop people taking any more, but in 1987, a local man found eight bottles in the wreck and sold them at auction for £4,000!

If you spot a normal-looking farmhouse in the northeast of Fife, you probably wouldn't realize that beneath it is a tunnel that leads to 2,230 sq m (24,000 sq ft) of accommodation and operations rooms. If there had been a nuclear war back in the late twentieth century, this is where Scotland would have been governed from. The bunker, built in 1953, is 30 m (100 ft) underground and is on two levels, each the size of two football pitches, one on top of the other. These days it's a museum called **Scotland's Secret Bunker**.

There are few islands on the east coast of Scotland, but you'll find some in the Firth of Forth. One of the most easily recognizable – because it can be seen from trains that pass over the Forth

Rail Bridge – is **Inchgarvie Island**. Its history goes back to the sixteenth century, when King James IV built a castle there. Between 1519 and 1671 it was used as a prison, and in 1580 some people suffering from the plague were also quarantined there to keep them away from others. During the First and Second World Wars, guns and military buildings protected the **Forth Bridge** and Rosyth Dockyard from air attack.

The **River Tay** is Scotland's longest river, with a length of 193 km (120 miles). It flows from the slopes of Ben Lui and enters the North Sea just beyond Dundee. In 1914, the Royal Naval Air Service opened a seaplane base on the river at Dundee to patrol the east coast of Scotland and it came into use again in the Second World War. In 1938, a special aircraft called the *Maia-Mercury*, which was a seaplane mounted on top of a flying boat, took off from the Tay and set a world-record distance flight of 9,728 km (6,045 miles) from Dundee to South Africa.

New Lanark is a tiny village of just sixty-five households surrounded by forests on the banks of the River Clyde. It was built in the eighteenth century to house workers for local cotton-spinning mills that were powered by water from the river. After the mill buildings stopped being used in the late 1960s, it became almost derelict, but it was saved by an organization that was created to look after the mills and the surrounding houses and repair them. Today, it's a stunning UNESCO World Heritage Site of "outstanding universal value" and attracts more than 300,000 visitors a year. Fun fact – it's where the author of this book (hello!) grew up.

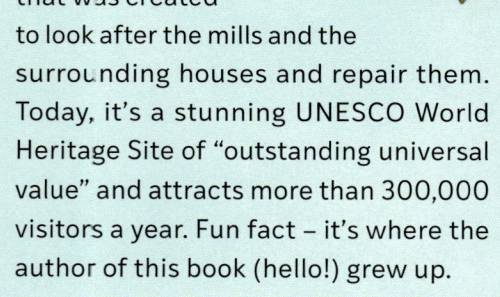

If you're out on a boat, keep your eyes peeled for something HUGE! The **basking shark** is the second largest fish on the planet, and can be found off the west coast of Scotland. Basking sharks can grow to 12 m (39 ft) – as long as a bus! – weigh up to 6 tonnes (13,200 lbs) and live for as long as one hundred years.

44

They baffle scientists by disappearing from the coast in winter. Nobody knows where they go, so if you see one hiding in the bushes at your local park, do drop the experts a line.

Two famous names associated with Edinburgh are ones the city might want to forget – **Burke and Hare**. In the early 1800s, Edinburgh was a great centre of anatomical research, meaning there was a high demand for human bodies to study. The only problem was, there weren't enough bodies to go round. Some criminals looking to cash in on the craze robbed graves and sold the bodies they dug up to surgeons to dissect, but two Irish men named William Burke and William Hare went a step further. They created new dead bodies by murdering people, which certainly saved them the effort of digging holes. It's thought they killed up to sixteen unsuspecting victims, before selling the bodies to surgeon Robert Knox for a tidy sum.

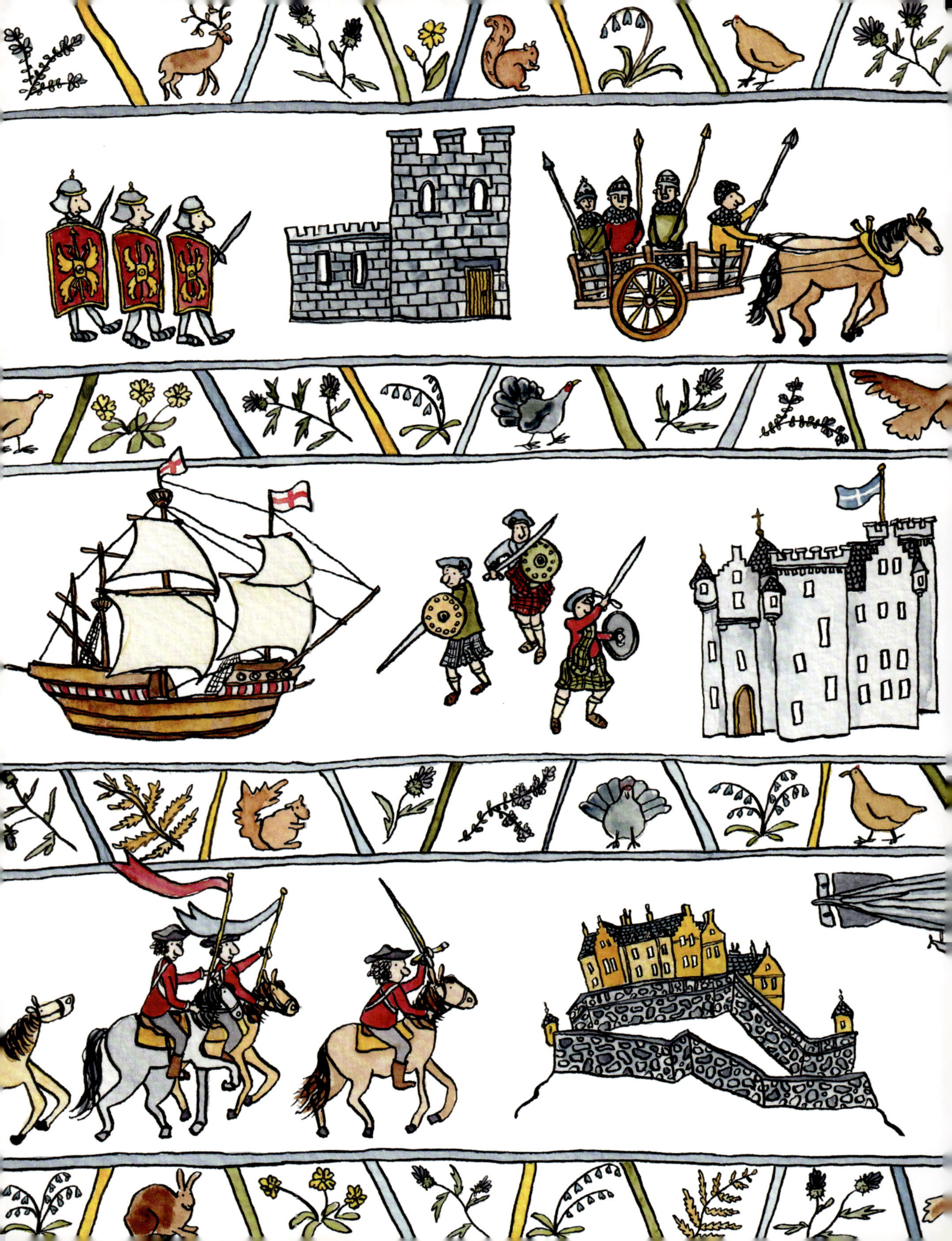

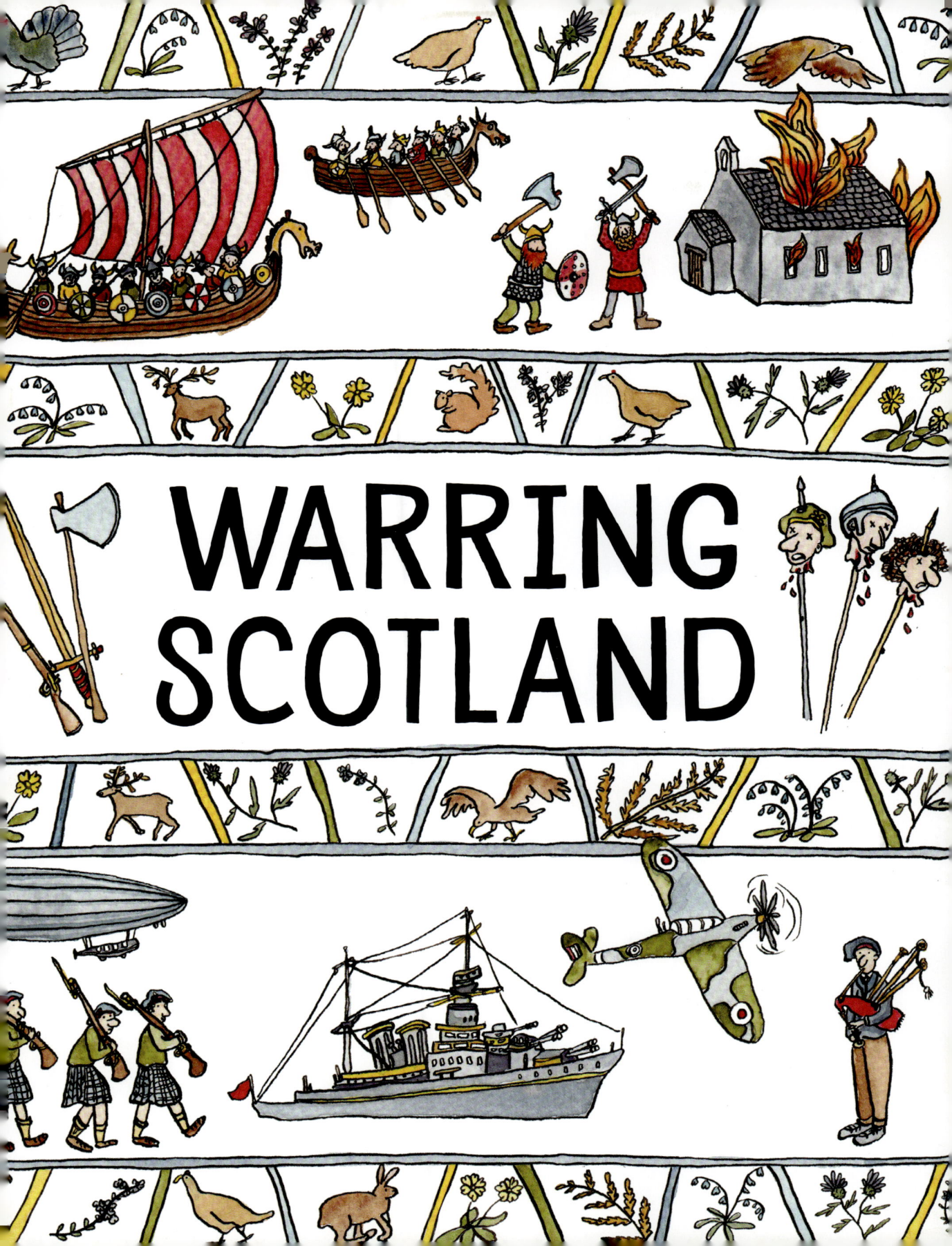

WARRING SCOTLAND

Map of Scotland

- Eilean Donan
- Battle of the Spoiling Dyke
- Battle of Gruinart
- Battle of the Shirts
- Siege of Dumbarton
- Battle of Largs

N E S W

SHETLAND ↗ 210 km (130 miles)

ORKNEY ISLANDS → 16 km (10 miles)

Scapa Flow

Battle of Culloden

Dunnottar Castle

Battle of Killiecrankie

Battle of Falkirk

Battle of the Clans

Battle of Stirling Bridge

Edinburgh Castle

Battle of Bannockburn

Tantallon Castle

Battle of Pinkie

Melrose Abbey

WARRING SCOTLAND

The people of Scotland have a long history of poking people with swords and being poked by other people with swords.

From ancient times right up until the last battle fought on Scottish soil – the **Battle of Culloden** in 1746 – there was usually someone fighting someone else somewhere in Scotland. From the Romans to the Vikings to the English, Scotland has had to fight off invaders for thousands of years – sometimes successfully, sometimes not so much. And that's just outsiders. When us Scots weren't fighting foreign armies, we could be found battling with each other, clan on clan.

The bloody history of Scotland is evident in the sheer number of castles here. There are estimated to be more than 1,500 castles dotted around the place. People don't build castles because they want plenty of room for their ping-pong table. They do it because they're worried about being attacked.

Sometimes it's those closest to you who you fight with the most, and England isn't known as the Auld Enemy ("auld" means "old") for nothing. Many of Scotland's bloodiest battles, such as Bannockburn and Falkirk, were fought against its much larger neighbour, and countless people on both sides died over the centuries during conflicts between the two countries.

Thankfully, nowadays battles between Scotland and England are fought on sporting fields, though the rivalry is still fierce and it can be painful if you're on the losing side.

THE CLANS

From McDonald to Armstrong, Campbell to MacLeod, Douglas to Sinclair and beyond – these names are all good Scottish clan names.

What's a clan? Imagine a family that has thousands and thousands of people in it and you're sort of in the right ballpark. You'd need a big living room if you were having a family get-together, put it that way.

The term "clan" really does mean "family" or "children" in Gaelic, but that doesn't actually mean everyone in the same clan was related to each other. People often adopted a clan surname to ensure protection and show they supported the clan.

Throughout Scottish history, fights, fall-outs and bloody battles were not uncommon between the various clans, with rivalry, betrayal, land disputes and a desire for power sparking conflicts down the years. Clan allegiance often meant more than allegiance to country – it was that strong.

Clans sometimes formed alliances, but when they didn't, things could get nasty. The **Battle of the Spoiling Dyke** took place in 1578 on the Isle of Skye between the MacLeods and the MacDonalds, who were sworn enemies at the time. One day, when the MacLeods gathered for a church service, a group of MacDonalds surrounded the church and set it on fire. All but one of those inside died. Before the MacDonalds could escape the island, more MacLeods arrived and slayed every one of them.

Nearly 200 years earlier in 1396, two clans – there have been arguments for hundreds of years over exactly which ones – fought each other in the **Battle of the Clans**, also known as the Battle of North Inch, in Perth. Somewhat bizarrely, the battle was staged to settle their differences – which means it was mutually arranged and fought in front of spectators, like a particularly bloody football match.

Thirty men from each clan were chosen to fight to the death. Many men fell, but one clan eventually took the upper hand and, when the last of the opposing clan left alive jumped in the River Tay, the remaining eleven warriors claimed victory.

An interesting side note is that at the beginning of the battle the clan that would go on to win was one man short, so a local blacksmith called **Hal o' the Wynd** said he'd join them for a small payment. He survived almost unscathed and, so the story goes, went on to start the Clan Gow, the Gaelic word for blacksmith.

VIKING INVADERS

If you think of Vikings as vicious warriors with horned helmets who invaded, raided and pillaged places, you'd only be partially right. Vikings didn't have horns on their helmets, you see – that was made up in the nineteenth century – but they definitely did more than their fair share of raiding and pillaging. Scotland was high on their bumper list of pillage targets.

However, the Vikings also came to stay. From the eighth century onwards, Vikings invaded and colonized Scottish islands – particularly Shetland and Orkney – and parts of the mainland. In the year AD 870, a Viking army laid siege to Dumbarton, which was the capital of the Kingdom of Alt Clut at the time. The siege lasted four months and ended when the defenders ran out of water. The Vikings captured them and sold them into slavery in Dublin.

Four hundred years later, an important battle brought the age of the Vikings in Scotland to an end. The **Battle of Largs** in 1263 began with King Haakon IV of Norway sailing an army to the west coast of Scotland. The Scottish king, Alexander III, delayed him by agreeing to talks – really, he was using the time to get his own army ready.

The Vikings were strong, but the Scottish weather was on Alexander's side, sending a storm that tore through Haakon's ships. The next day the forces met and there was a fierce fight on the beach. It was kind of a draw, with the Scots pulling back and the Vikings taking to their ships. But it wasn't long before Scandinavian control over Scotland started to diminish and the age of the Vikings was over.

ROBERT THE BRUCE AND WILLIAM WALLACE

When it comes to fighting for freedom, William Wallace is probably Scotland's best-known hero. He was born around 1270 and was one of the main leaders during the First War of Scottish Independence to end English rule in Scotland. He famously defeated Edward I's much larger English army at the **Battle of Stirling Bridge** in September 1297, but he was then defeated by Edward at the **Battle of Falkirk** in 1298. That didn't stop old William though – he kept on raiding the north of England and was given the title of Guardian of Scotland.

Wallace escaped for a while, but Edward wanted him dead, and he was finally captured in 1305. Edward had him hung, drawn and quartered – which means his body was chopped into four pieces – and his head was dipped in tar and popped on a sharp stick on top of **London Bridge**.

Another great Scottish hero from that time was **Robert the Bruce**, who managed to avoid the whole head-on-pointy-stick thing. He was king of Scotland from 1306 to 1329 and helped free Scotland from English rule by winning what is one of the most famous Scottish battles of all – the **Battle of Bannockburn** in 1314.

Edward II had marched a huge army up to Scotland, but Robert, with a force a fraction of the size, used clever tactics and rousing speeches to destroy Edward's knights, cavalry and infantry. Although independence didn't follow immediately, Bannockburn made it possible fourteen years later.

Robert died in June 1329 – his body is buried in Dunfermline Abbey, his heart is in **Melrose Abbey** (after being taken on the Crusades, which were a series of religious wars in the Middle East fought between Christians and Muslims between the eleventh and sixteenth centuries), and his internal organs were embalmed and sent to St Serf's Church in Dumbarton!

CASTLES

The closest most of us will ever get to owning a castle is building one made of sand on a beach. While you might be very pleased with it, it's not quite as impressive as the castles that you can find all over Scotland's landscape, from north to south and east to west.

Although later ones were built to show off, many are evidence of Scotland's turbulent, violent past and were vital defensive fortifications that protected the people and lands around them.

The most famous one of all is **Edinburgh Castle**. There's been a fort on the rock it sits on since Iron Age times, when the people back then recognized the strategic advantage of being perched so high up. The oldest part of the current castle is St Margaret's Chapel, built in the twelfth century, while the Great Hall was erected by James IV around 1511.

During the **Wars of Independence**, the castle was sometimes held by the Scots and sometimes by the English. In 1314, Thomas Randolph, nephew of Robert the Bruce, led a bold night raid to retake the castle. He and thirty of his men silently climbed up the castle rock, knowing they could tumble to their death at any moment or be found out by the troops above. When they made it to the top, they scaled the castle walls and fought the defenders inside, before burning it to the ground to prevent the English taking it back. Top stealthy work, chaps!

Just like Edinburgh Castle, **Stirling Castle** sits on volcanic rock. It's very important in Scotland's history, with battles such as Stirling Bridge and Bannockburn taking place nearby. It was also home to important royals, including Mary Queen of Scots and James VI and I (that's one person, by the way – he was James VI of Scotland and James I of England).

Stirling Castle was no stranger to sieges either. English leader Oliver Cromwell captured it in 1651 after besieging it. The final siege on the castle was led by Charles Edward Stuart, also known as Bonnie Prince Charlie, in around 1746.

Other incredible Scottish castles include the likes of Eilean Donan, Tantallon and Dunnottar.

Eilean Donan, in the north-west Highlands, is on an island where three great sea lochs meet. It once protected the lands around it from Viking raiders.

Tantallon in East Lothian is famed for its humongous 3.6-m- (12-ft-) thick walls. They still didn't stop it getting blown up by old Oliver Cromwell though.

Finally, **Dunnottar** looks like something from a King Arthur legend. It's perched on top of a 50-m (160-ft) rock surrounded on three sides by the North Sea. It has hosted the likes of William Wallace and Mary Queen of Scots, and saved the Honours of Scotland – the Scottish Crown Jewels – from that Oliver Cromwell (him again!).

BATTLES

You've probably had a few battles in your time. The great Battle of Who Should Tidy Up Your Stinky Socks that you had with your parents last week, for instance. Terrible though that was, it was nothing compared to the proper barneys that have taken place on Scottish soil over the years.

Let's begin by going way back in time. The **Battle of Mons Graupius** was fought in AD 83 between the Roman invaders and a Pictish army. No one is sure exactly where it took place, though it was probably somewhere in the north-east of Scotland. The Roman historian Tacitus claimed that 10,000 Pictish lives were lost at a cost of only 360 Roman army troops, although it's very likely that he was exaggerating. What a wee fibber!

Some battles have names that sound almost cute ... though they're anything but! The **Battle of Pinkie** was fought on 10 September 1547, on the banks of the River Esk near Musselburgh in East Lothian. It was the last battle between Scotland and England before the Union of the Crowns, when King James VI of Scotland also became James I of England. In Scotland, the battle became known as Black Saturday – a bit of a clue that it didn't go well for the Scottish army. At one point, the Scots were under heavy fire on three sides – from English ships off the coast, and from both cannons and archers on land. The Scots retreated but were slaughtered or drowned as they tried to swim back across the river.

One of the most famous battles is the one fought at Culloden. It took place on 16 April 1746, as part of the final **Jacobite rising**, and was the last pitched battle (which means it was organized ahead of time) on British soil. The Jacobites wanted to restore the House of Stuart to the British throne, with their army made up of many Scottish clans aiming to make their leader, Bonnie Prince Charlie, king. Charlie's army gathered to take on the Duke of Cumberland's government troops at Culloden Moor, near Inverness. In less than an hour around 1,300 men lay dead or wounded on the battlefield – 1,250 of them Jacobites. It was a terrible defeat.

WOULD YOU BELIEVE IT?

The first German aircraft shot down on British soil during the Second World War was claimed by ace Scottish pilot **Archie McKellar** over Humbie, near Edinburgh. In October 1939, he was flying his Spitfire when he got the Heinkel HE-111 bomber in his sights. McKellar went on to become a war hero, being awarded the Distinguished Flying Cross and Bar and the Distinguished Service Order for shooting down twenty-one enemy aircraft in one day. Sadly, like so many others on all sides, he was killed in action after being shot down in 1940.

As well as being home to Scottish and British troops, **Edinburgh Castle** has also been used to hold prisoners of war – not always successfully. You can still see the hole that forty-nine French prisoners hacked in a wall in 1811. After they scurried through the hole, they used ropes to escape down the south crag of the castle rock. All but one made it off the rock but were then recaptured!

The **Battle of the Shirts** in 1544 was one of the bloodiest battles fought between the clans. It is said that it earned its name after the men stripped off their heavy tartan in the hot July sun. Clan Fraser and Clan Grant took on the MacDonalds, Camerons and Donalds, and apparently just thirteen men survived out of the 800 who started the battle.

The first ever air raid on Scottish soil took place on 2 April 1916, when Edinburgh was bombed by two German airships called **Zeppelins**. Bombs started landing in Leith, which is home to docks, shortly before midnight. It must have been confusing and terrifying and, although the attack only lasted thirty-five minutes, twenty-three bombs were dropped, thirteen people were killed and twenty-four were injured.

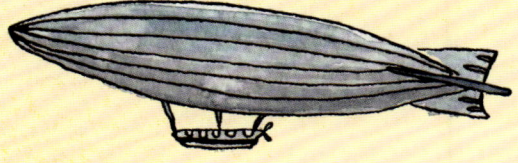

83
Battle of Mons Graupius

600
First fort built on Castle Rock, site of Edinburgh Castle

870
Siege of Dumbarton

1263
Battle of Largs

1296–1328
Wars of Independence

1544
Battle of the Shirts

1547
Battle of Pinkie

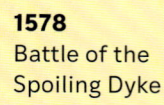

1578
Battle of the Spoiling Dyke

1598
Battle of Gruinart

1651
Siege of Stirling Castle

Not all Scottish battles were fought only by humans. According to legend, **the Battle of Gruinart** on the island of Islay in 1598 featured a furious fairy. Sir Lachlan Mor MacLean, the 14th Chief of Duart, was to do battle with his nephew Sir James MacDonald of Islay. Just before the fighting began, Dubh Sith – the Black Fairy, whose father was human and mother was a fairy – arrived from the nearby island of Jura to offer his services as an archer to MacLean. But Sir Lachlan told the fairy to get lost. This turned out to be a very bad idea. Angry at the snub, Dubh Sith joined the other side and, as you can probably guess, shot the arrow that killed MacLean. So, if a fairy ever offers to do you a favour, just say yes.

1297
Battle of Stirling Bridge

1298
Battle of Falkirk

1314
Battle of Bannockburn

1396
Battle of the Clans/Battle of North Inch

1490–1600
Stirling Castle built

1689
Battle of Killiecrankie

1746
Battle of Culloden

1916
First ever air raid on Scottish soil

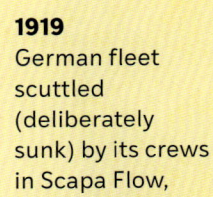

1919
German fleet scuttled (deliberately sunk) by its crews in Scapa Flow, Orkney Islands

1939
First German bomber of the Second World War shot down near Edinburgh

Mons Meg is an enormous cannon that can be found at **Edinburgh Castle**. Given to King James II in 1457, it weighs 6 tonnes (13,200 lb), could fire a stone cannonball up to 3 km (2 miles) and was so heavy it could only be moved around 5 km (3 miles) a day. When Mary Queen of Scots married in 1558, Mons Meg fired in celebration and the stone landed in what is now the Royal Botanic Garden.

Tantallon Castle may have been a medieval fortress, but it played an important part in the Second World War as well. In 1944, captured German radars based at the castle were used to train RAF bomber crews to deceive the enemy. The night before the D-Day landings in France, thin strips of aluminium foil were dropped to make the German radar operators think a big navy fleet was approaching – a trick that had been perfected in the waters off Tantallon Castle.

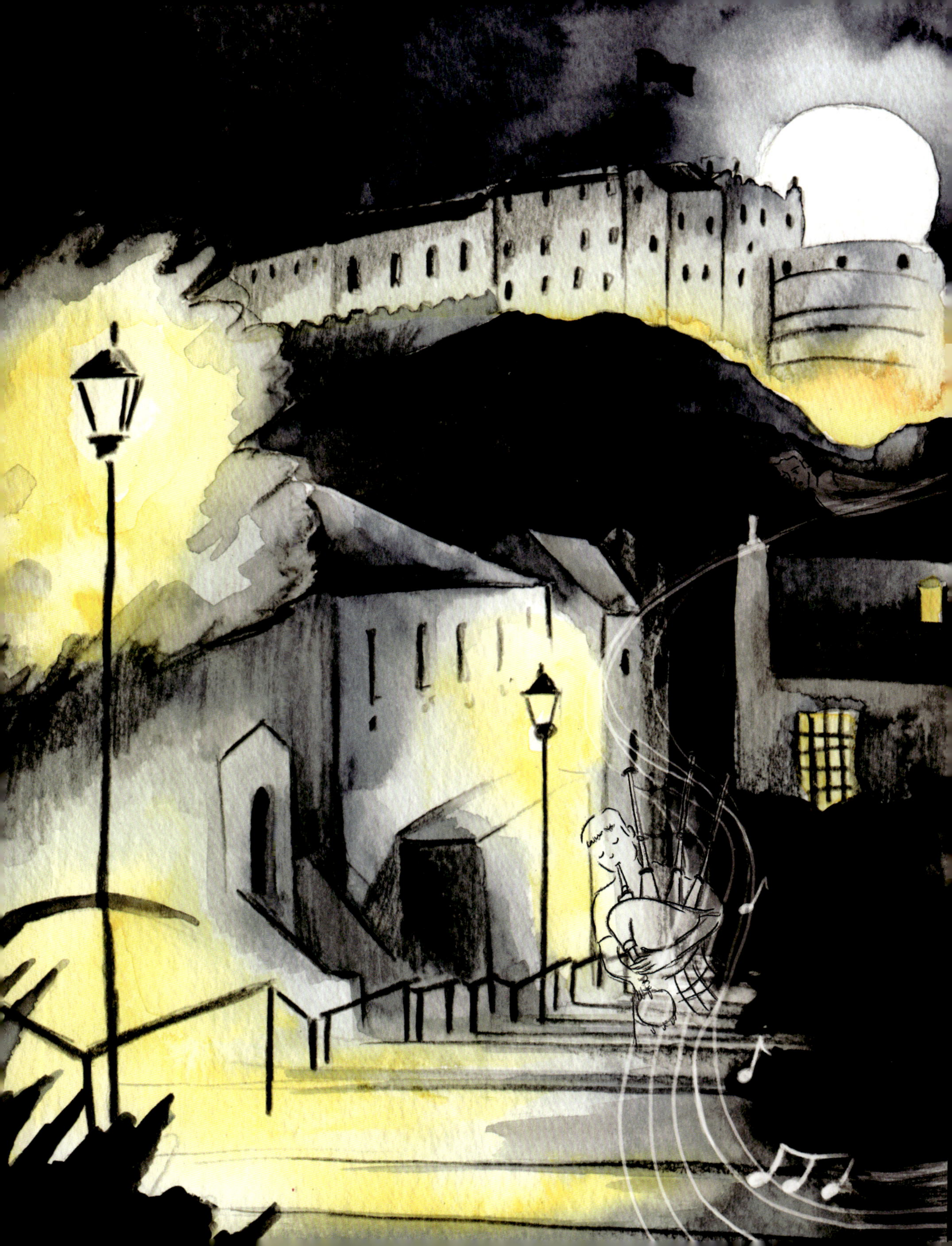

HAUNTED SCOTLAND

SHETLAND 210 km (130 miles)

Skall House, Orkney

ORKNEY 16 km (10 miles)

Dunrobin Castle

Crathes Castle

Drum Castle

House of Dun

Craigievar Castle

Forest of Rothiemurchus

Battle of Killiecrankie

Ghost Car, Skye

RAF Montrose

St Andrews Cathedral

Tay Bridge Disaster

Falkland Palace

Alloa Tower

Mary King's Close

Edinburgh Castle

Rosslyn Chapel

A75 road Dumfries to Annan

King's Theatre, Glasgow

Linlithgow Palace

Culzean Castle

Glencoe Massacre

Brodick Castle

Scotland Street School

Inveraray Castle

HAUNTED SCOTLAND

The history – and present – of Scotland is awash with terrible tales of ghostly goings on and spooky spirits creeping people out. The Scots love a good ghost story and can be a superstitious bunch at times. For instance, seeing three swans flying together is said to be a sign of impending disaster. And farmers in the north-east are particularly concerned by the appearance of a black-faced sheep, which is said to bring bad luck.

On the flip side of the luck coin, white heather, which is far less common than the purple variety, is said to be a good thing. The origins of that superstition come from a Celtic legend dating from the third century. Malvina, the daughter of warrior-poet Ossian, wept after finding out her true love had died in battle and her tears turned the purple heather white. She said, "Although it is the symbol of my sorrow, may the white heather bring good fortune to all who find it." After that, so the story goes, clansmen would wear white heather in battle, though wearing a suit of white armour would probably have been better.

But it's ghosts that really capture the Scots' imagination. And with so many crumbling castles, dark winding streets and old mansions kicking around, it's no surprise there are spirits aplenty.

HOUSE OF DUN

We've all lost things at times. You've probably lost your games console controller even though you literally put it down right there only one minute ago! But have you ever lost your head? We're really hoping the answer is no. But that's what seems to have happened to one unfortunate horseman who is said to haunt the **House of Dun** near Montrose.

While it might be a beautiful eighteenth-century laird's (lord's) home set in stunning scenery, it holds dark, murderous secrets… A headless horseman is rumoured to roam the lanes of the Dun estate at night, looking to take revenge for his plight on unwary travellers. So if you're travelling, be wary. And don't mention hats, it'll just upset him.

The horseman is not the only spirit in the local area. If you hear the sound of spooky strings being strummed, it could be the harpist who is said to have been murdered long ago in the wooded Den of Dun. Don't expect the latest up-tempo pop tunes. Then there's the knight who returned home from the Crusades to discover his friend had tricked his wife into marrying him. The knight was a bit miffed, so he started a sword fight and ended up skewering his ex-friend on a yew tree. It's no wonder the knight's ghost has been hanging around for centuries.

CRATHES CASTLE

A lot of castles and stately homes have a ghost – usually a lady – who is described as one colour or another. But **Crathes Castle** has two. The first is the White Lady. Crathes was built on land given to the Burnett family by none other than Robert the Bruce in 1323. To begin with, the family lived on an artificial island in a loch before they moved into the castle, which was finished in 1596.

The legend goes that the **White Lady** is the spirit of a woman named Bertha who fell in love with Alexander Burnett, who was the young laird at the time. They would have been married, if it wasn't for the fact that the laird's mum, Lady Agnes, didn't think Bertha was good enough for him. So, she poisoned her. Talk about overreacting! It's said that on the anniversary of her death each year, the White Lady walks on a track near the castle.

If white isn't your colour, there's a **Green Lady**, too – and even Queen Victoria claims to have seen her!

Who she was is shrouded in mystery, but one tale suggests that she was the daughter of one of the lairds, and had a baby with a stable boy. The laird was furious and, shortly after he found out, the girl and the baby disappeared. Whatever the truth, these days the Green Lady appears either as a young woman carrying a baby or a green orb that disappears into a fireplace where, centuries later, a baby's skeleton was found under the hearth.

KILLIECRANKIE

Enough of castles for now. Let's get some fresh air in the great outdoors – on a haunted battlefield to be exact. Hey! Why are you running away? Come back here!

On 27 July 1689, at the **Battle of Killiecrankie**, which is just north of Pitlochry, 4,000 government troops were defeated by a 3,000-strong rebel Highland army, led by Viscount Dundee, who was known as Bonnie Dundee. Obviously, one classic aspect of battles is that lots of soldiers often end up dead, unfortunately, so it's not surprising that some battlefields are said to be haunted.

At Killiecrankie, the whole terrible battle is replayed by ghostly warriors on certain days.

In more recent times, one woman claimed she saw the battle and its aftermath, while other people have claimed they've spotted apparitions of long-gone soldiers. On the anniversary of the battle, the area has been seen to glow red and the sound of footsteps can be heard as the government army march to meet their gruesome end. People have even insisted they've had a hair-raising meeting with a floating head. Perhaps it could be introduced to the headless horseman at the House of Dun. The perfect match!

MARY KING'S CLOSE

Nobody likes feeling unwell. Runny nose? No, thanks. Upset tummy? Yuck! But for the unfortunate residents of one Edinburgh street, not only did they have to contend with the **Great Plague** of 1645, but some were locked inside their homes, to protect others from catching the disease.

terrible death, although a doctor did try to save as many as possible by spearing their boils and sealing them with a red-hot poker! In the eighteenth century, part of the close was demolished and buried, with new buildings constructed over the top, leaving it sealed underground for hundreds of years.

Now it's a tourist attraction ... but it seems some of its former residents are reluctant to leave. The best-known spectre is a young girl called Annie, who is said to haunt one of the rooms in the close. She's been seen by many people, and there's one room she's said to haunt in particular. Psychics and mediums (that's people who say they can communicate with the dead) say she was trapped in the street in 1645, when the plague was at its worst.

It's said she's forlornly looking for her lost dolly, so visitors leave dolls, toys and sweets to cheer her up. Just to be clear – pretending you're a seventeenth-century ghost to get people to give you toys and sweets is not a good idea.

A "close" is a Scottish word for a narrow alley between buildings. **Mary King's Close**, which is just off Edinburgh's famous Royal Mile, was inhabited during the seventeenth century when there was a terrible outbreak of bubonic plague. Many poor people were quarantined in the close and died a

EDINBURGH CASTLE'S GHOSTS

Edinburgh Castle is built on an extinct volcano, right in the centre of the city, and is bursting at its stony seams with ghosts, according to some people. One of the best known is the **little piper boy** who, centuries ago, was sent into a dark, hidden tunnel beneath the castle to see where it went. He was told to play his bagpipes as he explored, so the men aboveground could track where he was. All was going well until, suddenly, the pipes stopped. The boy had completely disappeared and was never seen again.

But he was heard again ... or at least his ghost was. Nowadays people report hearing the faint skirl of bagpipes from beneath their feet as the little piper boy wanders the lonely tunnels below.

Another instrument-based haunting is the headless drummer boy. The story goes that, in 1650, a boy without a head was seen on the castle walls playing a spooky *rat-a-tat-tat* on his drum. It's said that when he's sighted, the castle is in danger. While he's waiting for the next threat to the castle, perhaps he should get together with the piper boy and start a band. Watch out for them on Britain's Ghosts Got Talent!

The last spectre we'll mention isn't seen or heard ... but he is smelled. One poor prisoner who was held in the castle's dungeons decided to try to escape by hiding in a barrow full of dung. It was a great idea, until it was emptied over the side of the castle and down onto the rocks below. If dying counts as escaping, his cunning plan was a great success! In the centuries since then, visitors have said his smelly spirit tries to push them off the walls, accompanied by the tangy reek of horse poop! So, take a peg for your nose and hold on tight next time you visit the castle.

Hundreds of years ago, superstitious folk would hide things in their houses to try to keep naughty spirits away. They'd put personal objects, like gloves, broken pottery, clothes, glass and clay pipes, in spaces in walls, fireplaces, under floorboards and in attics. Rather than trying to ward off evil spirits, the items were intended to lead the spirits on a wild goose chase and make them latch on to the objects, rather than the people who lived in the house. To be honest, if the spirits couldn't tell the difference between a glove and a person, they probably deserved to be tricked.

WOULD YOU BELIEVE IT?

Ghosts are practically queuing up to haunt castles and old houses, but there aren't many hanging around bridges. But then, not many have experienced terrible tragedies like that of the **Tay Bridge**, which crosses the river from Fife to Dundee. The Tay Bridge disaster on 28 December 1879 is one of the worst bridge catastrophes in Scottish history. A train full of people was crossing during a terrible storm that had weakened the bridge's central section. With a tearing crash, the bridge collapsed and the train plummeted into the icy river below, killing everyone on board, around seventy-five people.

Now it is said that on the anniversary of the disaster, a ghostly train can be seen crossing where the old bridge would once have stood. When it reaches the point where the section collapsed, it disappears!

Bridges aren't the only haunted travel routes in Scotland. The A75 in Dumfriesshire is said to be one of the most haunted roads in Scotland. Sightings include screaming hags and eyeless phantoms!

Do you find your school truly terrifying? Maybe that's because the custard served up in the school canteen is enough to send shivers down anyone's spine. But at **Scotland Street School** in Glasgow, there are spookier things to worry about. It was designed by famous Scottish architect Charles Rennie Mackintosh, but while it might look bonny, it can be creepy too. Nowadays the building houses a museum that shows what life was like in a Victorian school, and staff have claimed objects move on their own, footsteps echo down empty hallways and the sound of spooky laughter can be heard from the upper floors.

Rosslyn Chapel was built for the St Clair family in the fifteenth century and is a very cool place. Almost every stone surface is covered with mysterious carvings and symbols that have puzzled and intrigued people for centuries. Some people even believe the Holy Grail is hidden somewhere in the chapel. It's a beautiful place, but you probably wouldn't want to spend the night there alone. It's said flames can be seen flickering in mid-air in the burial vault of the chapel whenever one of the Sinclair family is about to die. There's also a story that the apprentice stonemason who carved the famous Apprentice Pillar was murdered by his teacher, which is pretty harsh. The poor lad can sometimes be seen or heard wandering the chapel.

One of the most infamous and bloody events in Scottish history, the **Glencoe Massacre**, took place on 13 February 1692 in a glen in the Highlands. The tragic tale begins with a troop of soldiers pretending to be friendly visitors. They were taken in and offered hospitality by the people of the Clan MacDonald. But in the dead of night, the soldiers got up and mercilessly attacked their hosts while they slept in their beds, murdering thirty-eight men, women and children. Those who escaped fled to the mountains, but died in

74

the freezing cold. Not surprisingly after such a terrible crime, people claim the ghosts of the MacDonalds can still be seen and heard. Some people say they have seen the slaughter being replayed, while others say they've heard blood-curdling screams in the glen.

Seath Mor Sgor Fhiaclach (just call him Steve if you can't manage the pronunciation) was a fourteenth-century chief of the Clan Shaw. He was a formidable warrior, and stood well over 2 m (6 ft) tall, until he died and started lying down a lot more than standing. His grave can be found in the **Forest of Rothiemurchus**, near Aviemore, and is protected by five cursed stones. Those who touch them meet a grisly end – and they are now covered with a metal cage to stop visitors giving them an ill-advised rub. On top of that, some people have spoken of a gigantic ghostly figure challenging them to a battle at the graveside. If they accept, they're fine and the figure disappears. But if they show fear, they are never seen again. In other words, stay away from big Steve's grave.

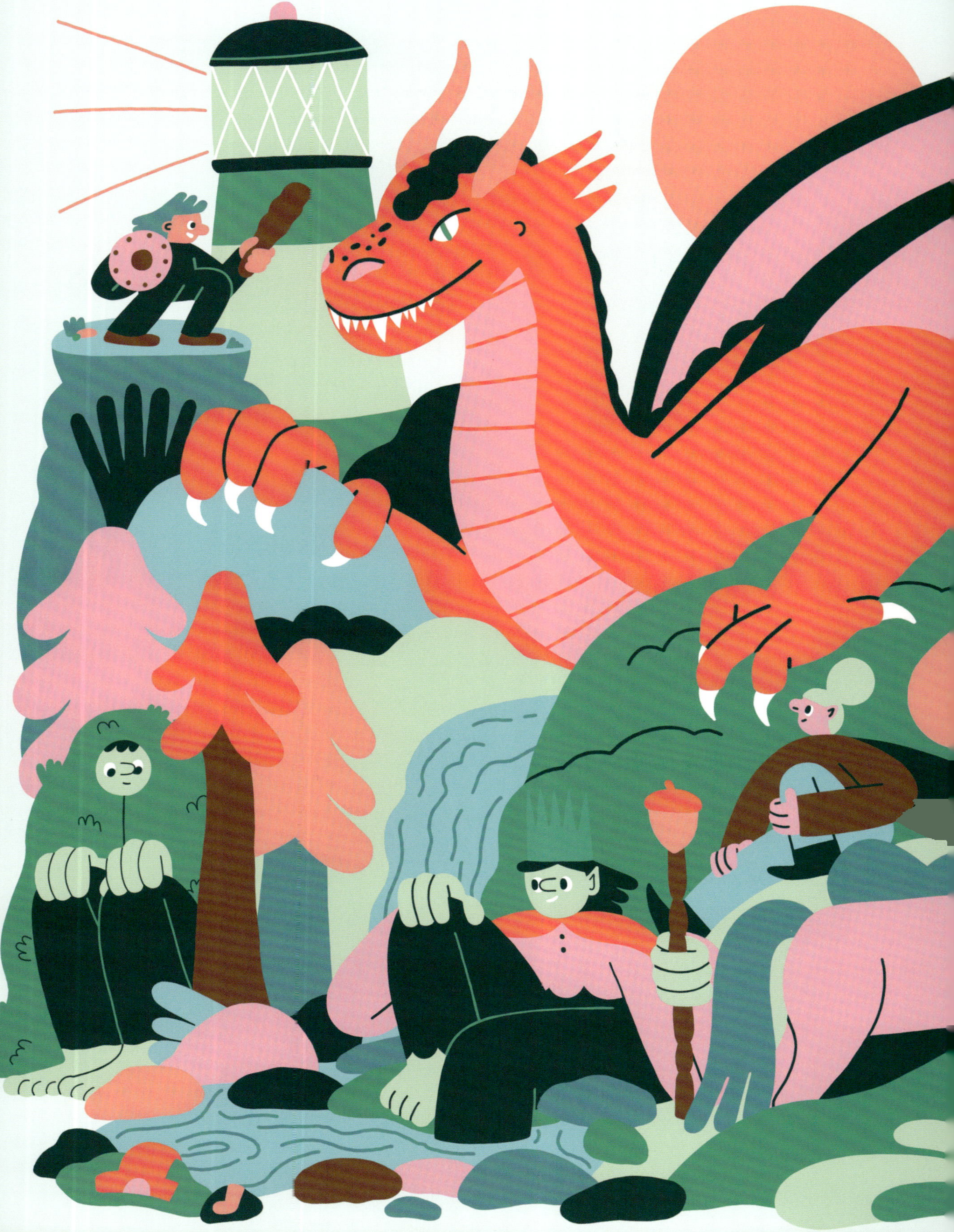

LEGENDARY SCOTLAND

- Flannan Isles
- Callanish Stones
- The Minch
- Fairy Glen
- Ghillie Dhu
- Fairy Pools
- Gairloch
- Fingal's Cave
- Corryvreckan Whirlpool

ORKNEY 16 km (10 miles)

Clootie Well

Stoor Worm

River Spey

SHETLAND 210 km (130 miles)

Loch Ness

Glenmore Forest Park

Pittenweem

Loch Earn

Devil's Pulpit

Standing Stones of Lundin

North Berwick

Arthur's Seat

Beltane Fire Festival

Gorbals / Necropolis

LEGENDARY SCOTLAND

Life is full of mystery and magic. There's the mystery of whether your headteacher is actually human or not, and it can only be magic when your favourite stuff disappears from your bedroom and reappears in your brother's or sister's room.

Scotland's history and landscape is rich with myths and legends of fairy folk, monsters, giants and witches. You can barely step out the door in Scotland without finding yourself in an enchanted place – just be careful you don't stand on a fairy, as they're pretty small and quite hard to see. Speaking of fairies, if you like those little creatures, you should make a beeline for the Isle of Skye. There you'll find the **Fairy Pools** and the **Fairy Glen** – two fairy hangouts for the price of one! The Fairy Pools are enchanting rock pools filled with translucent spring water surrounded by waterfalls, while the Fairy Glen has an otherworldly feel with rocky outcrops, small green hills and lochans (little pond-like lochs).

The reason for the fairy place names, according to legend, is that a local Clan MacLeod chief married a fairy princess. It is also said that the Fairy Pools attracted selkies at night – more on those critters later.

You might also want to pay a visit to the little loch of An Lochan Uaine (which means "The Green Loch") in **Glenmore Forest Park**. Its stunning emerald waters are said to have been created when **Dòmhnall Mòr**, the king of the pixies, washed his clothes in it. Next time you turn your bath water a weird colour, just tell your mum and dad you're pixie royalty.

Read on for more myths, magic and mystery.

FAIRY FOLK

We've already mentioned the pools and glen of Skye, but fairies can be found (or rather, not found) all over Scotland. You might think of fairies as cute little sprites with fluttering wings and glittery outfits – all lovely and sweet – but some fairies can be bad news.

In many Scottish folk tales, fairies can be at least a bit bothersome, if not downright evil. Ancient stories tell of fairy folk stealing human babies and leaving changelings in their place. A changeling is a strange fairy child that looks like the original baby, but acts oddly and might even have a little beard and long teeth (bit of a giveaway, those ones). Suggesting that your little brother or sister might be a changeling may not go down well with your parents.

Other types of fairies are really nasty. **Baobhan Sith** are vampire fairies who drink their victims' blood, for instance. Offering them a banana milkshake instead will not help.

Of course, not all fairies are bad. Some are jolly helpful. Brownies, for instance, are said to have a pleasant nature. These small brown elves help with chores in Scottish homes while people are asleep. But you have to be good to them or they'll disappear, which is fair enough.

Another mythical fairy type is **Ghillie Dhu**. It is said that he lived in a forest in north-west Scotland, dressed in clothes of moss and leaves and only came out at night. That might sound a wee bit creepy, but he was a kindly sprite who helped children when they were lost in the woods. One such child was little Jessie Macrae, who got lost in the forest on a summer night. Ghillie Dhu looked after her until morning, and then led her home. A local landowner and his wealthy chums set out to try to capture Ghillie Dhu, but he couldn't be found and was never seen again.

KELPIES

Horses are great! They've been an important part of life in Scotland for hundreds of years, helping people travel far and wide and farm their crops. The only time horses are not so great is when they're **kelpies** – unless you think being dragged underwater and eaten is great...

To be fair to horses, kelpies are actually Scottish water spirits that usually appear in the form of horses, haunting streams and rivers and waiting for unsuspecting prey. They may look tame and peaceful to begin with, but touch their skin and you'll stick to it! The kelpie will then gallop into the water, taking you with it.

One Scottish folk tale tells of a kelpie luring nine children onto its back. A tenth child stroked its nose and his finger became stuck. He managed to escape only by cutting off his own finger, but the other nine were never seen again!

82

If you're worried a horse could be a kelpie, check its legs. Kelpies' hooves are the wrong way round. If you're in Aberdeenshire, a kelpie's mane is made from serpents, and in the **River Spey** the kelpie may be white and will sing to tempt you onto its back. Wonky hooves are one thing, but if you see a horse with snakes on its head or a pale pony belting out a popular show tune, you should already be running away. A quick word of advice: if you do come across a kelpie, it does have one weak spot – its bridle. If you can manage to grab a kelpie's bridle, you'll control it and any other kelpie.

WITCHES

Nowadays, you're most likely to experience witchy stuff in the fancy dress aisle of your local supermarket around Halloween. You're probably thinking green faces, wands, flying broomsticks and black cats. But hundreds of years ago in Scotland the people who were called witches were just ordinary people, usually (though not always) women.

The story of witches in Scottish history is sad and shameful. Terrifying not for us, but for the poor folk who were accused of witchcraft and then tortured and executed. Things started getting really bad in the late sixteenth century, when over 1,000 people were killed because it was believed they were witches.

One famous case took place around 1590, when it was claimed a group of women and men from East Lothian had met the devil and magically created a storm to try to sink the ship that the king, James VI, was sailing in. King James clearly believed this nonsense, because he examined the accused himself and personally saw to it that at least two of them were horribly tortured and burned at the stake.

Many more suffered the same fate, with terrible devices like thumbscrews and iron masks called "branks" used to make completely innocent people confess to witchcraft and even give the names of other innocent people. The end result was often death for them and those they'd named.

Men employed as "witch prickers" travelled around Scotland jabbing accused women with needles until they found a spot that didn't bleed – the "sure sign" of a witch. Long after this disgraceful job died out, it was discovered some of the needles were blunt and designed to disappear into the handle, only giving the impression that the woman had been pricked and not bled. Though the wrongs that were done to these people can never be righted, in 2022 the Scottish Government issued an official apology to the thousands of women and men who were persecuted as witches in Scotland.

SELKIES

The wonderful thing about people is that everyone's face looks different. We have all sizes of ears, noses and mouths, a variety of eye colours and hairstyles, different hues of skin and our heads aren't all the same shape. However, if you ever meet someone who literally has a seal's face, you would be forgiven for being a bit freaked out.

If this ever happens, chances are they're a **selkie**'s child. What's a selkie, you ask? In Scottish mythology, selkies are beings who can change from a seal to a human. All they have to do is shed their seal skin and – shazam! – they're a person. Tales of selkies originated in the Northern Isles of Orkney and Shetland, although they can also be found on the west coast of Scotland as well as Ireland, Scandinavia, Iceland and Cornwall. It was said that if a man stole a female selkie's seal skin while she was in human form, he could make her his wife. However, she would always long for the sea and her true selkie form, and if she ever discovered her seal skin again, she would immediately disappear back into the water, which seems entirely understandable.

Selkies could also be male, and there's a tale of an Orkney woman who fell in love with a handsome selkie chap. Whenever she wanted to summon him, all she had to do was cry seven tears into the sea and he would come.

It was said that children who were born from a human parent and a selkie parent had webbed hands and feet, like a seal, and in one tale from the Northern Isles, a woman gives birth to a son with a seal's face after falling for a selkie man. Another family of selkie descendants had green, cracked skin that had a fishy odour. So if you have a seal's face and smell faintly of herring, you should probably ask your mum and dad some questions.

THE LOCH NESS MONSTER

Most countries have tales of monsters and strange creatures, but there are few as famous as the **Loch Ness monster**, or Nessie as she is sometimes known. This mysterious monster has a history that goes back centuries. Some believe she's a plesiosaur, a type of marine reptile from the age of the dinosaurs that has been extinct for 66 million years.

The first written report of a monster in the loch appears in AD 565. In it, the author claimed the beast had a nibble at someone who was swimming in the water and was getting ready to chomp another man when St Columba, an Irish missionary who saw the attack, ordered the beast to "go back".

Over the centuries, the monster was seen now and again, until a famous sighting in 1933 sparked the modern-day Nessie craze. In April that year, a couple saw a huge dragon-like creature crossing the road in front of their car and disappearing into the water.

That December, a monster hunter claimed to have found enormous footprints on the side of the loch. It looked like Nessie could be real! But then experts at the Natural History Museum concluded that an umbrella stand with a hippopotamus leg base had been used to make the tracks. Unless Nessie owns a weird umbrella stand, it definitely wasn't her.

Then in 1934, a surgeon took the most famous photograph of all, which showed the monster's small head and long neck popping out of the water. Since then, millions of people from around the world have flocked to the loch in the hope of catching a glimpse. Over the years, scientists have carried out several sonar expeditions to try to locate Nessie, but she's never been found. Most recently it's been suggested giant eels could be behind the sightings.

Is Nessie real? That's up to you to decide...

WOULD YOU BELIEVE IT?

If you visit Dundee, keep an eye out for dragons. You'll find a statue of one in the city centre, and if you're very eagle-eyed – or should that be dragon-eyed – you can spot one on top of the spire of St Andrews Church. The city's coat of arms even features two dragons. Why the obsession with the winged creatures? It all stems from a local folk tale of a farmer and his nine daughters. The farmer sent his eldest daughter to gather water from a nearby well, but she didn't come back. So he sent his

86

second oldest daughter, and then his third oldest, and so on until they'd all vanished. When he went to investigate – a bit late if you ask me – he was horrified to find a huge dragon coiled around their bodies. The farmer called on his neighbours to help, and a young man named Martin slayed the dragon using only a wooden club. And that is why you'll find dragons in Dundee.

Another big beastie is the **Stoor Worm**. If you're thinking of a little pink wriggly thing, think again. The Stoor Worm was a gigantic sea serpent from the folklore of the Orkneys.

Its terrible breath could destroy crops and kill humans and farm animals alike. Every Saturday at sunrise, the Stoor Worm would yawn nine times with its gaping mouth and demand a meal of seven young women. It was finally slain by Assipattle, the youngest son of a local farmer. As it died, its teeth fell out to become the islands of Orkney, Shetland and the Faroes, and its body became Iceland. You'd better be nice to worms in your garden, just in case they're related...

How's this for creepy? In 1836, a group of young boys were out on **Arthur's Seat**, the hill near the centre of Edinburgh, when they came across seventeen tiny coffins hidden in a cave. Each coffin contained a small wooden figure dressed in specially made clothes. To this day, nobody knows why they were there or what they mean.

of Scotland in the twelfth century and was shown with gold chains wrapped around it – possibly meant to symbolize that Scottish kings were so powerful they could tame the untameable.

The **Gorbals** area of Glasgow was rife with poverty back in the 1950s, but despite the tough conditions, the children of the area clearly had a vivid imagination. Rumours started circulating that a 2-m (7-ft) vampire with iron teeth was lurking in the **Southern Necropolis**, a big cemetery nearby. Worried it was preying on children, and ignored by adults, a huge mob of the youngsters set out to find the bloodsucker one day in 1954. Hundreds of the Gorbals children descended on the Necropolis, seeking the creepy vampire with metal gnashers. The police were called, but the children wouldn't budge until a local headteacher finally dispersed the crowd.

What do you think Scotland's national animal is? A majestic golden eagle, perhaps, or a leaping salmon? You're wrong! Our national animal is something much more magical – the unicorn! In Celtic mythology, the unicorn is a symbol of purity and power. Unicorns are also notoriously independent and hard to conquer – so you can see why it was a powerful symbol in Scotland's turbulent past. The unicorn was first introduced to the royal coat of arms

The kelpies inland might be bad enough, but you really don't want to meet the ones that are said to inhabit the stretch of water between the northern Outer Hebrides and the Scottish mainland. These guys are storm kelpies – otherwise known as the **Blue Men of the Minch** – and are on the lookout for boats to sink and sailors to drown. They look pretty much like humans … apart from the fact they're blue. When the weather's good, they lie asleep on or just below the surface of the water. But they have the power to cause storms that sink ships. The tales go that they shout two lines of poetry to ships' captains. If the skipper can't complete the verse, they'll get that sinking feeling.

One of Scotland's greatest sea mysteries is the missing lighthouse keepers of the **Flannan Isles**. One night, the crew of a boat called the *Hesperus* noticed there was no beam coming from the lighthouse on the little island, 30 km (20 miles) west of Lewis and Harris. When they went to investigate, they found a meal lying untouched on the table, just waiting to be eaten, but there was absolutely no trace of the three lighthouse keepers. The mystery was never solved, though it was concluded that perhaps the men were washed away by a wave. But others suspect something altogether more mythical: sea monsters. Perhaps those blue men decided to pay the lighthouse a visit…

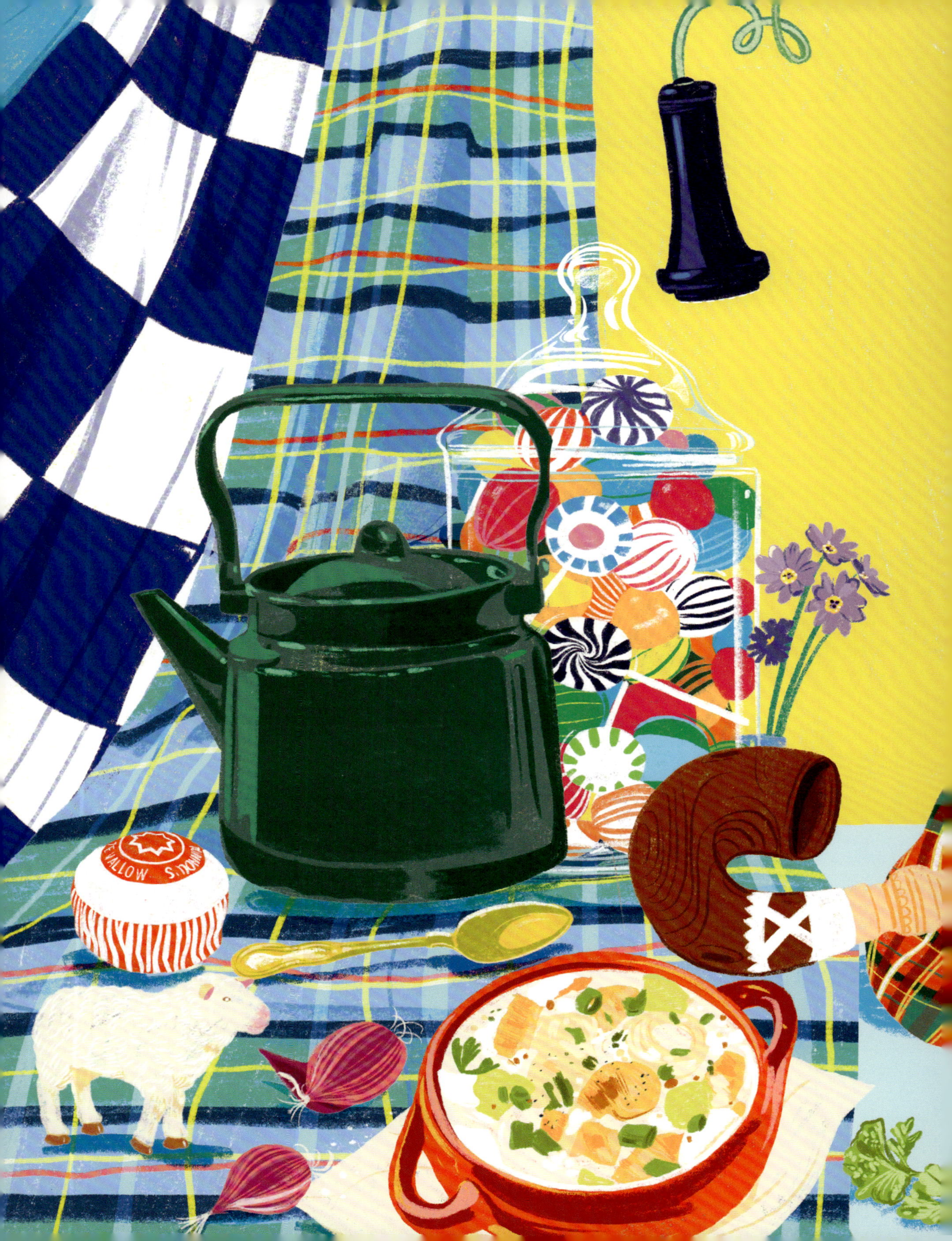

THE CULTURE OF SCOTLAND

Museum & Tasglann nan Eilean

Inverness (Karen Gillan)

Tobermory (Balamory)

Helensburgh (J.L. Baird)

Up Helly Aa

| ORKNEY | 16 km (10 miles) |
| SHETLAND | 210 km (130 miles) |

Cullen

Braemar Highland Games

V&A Dundee

Panopticon Music Hall, Glasgow

Old Course, St Andrews

Dunblane (Andy Murray)

Edinburgh (A. G. Bell)

Royal Yacht Britannia

Cumbernauld (IRN-BRU Factory)

Murrayfield

Hampden Park

Darvel (A. Fleming)

THE CULTURE OF SCOTLAND

Who are you? This sounds like an easy question – you'll probably just say your name. But wait! Who you are is so much more than your name. It's everything that influences you – everything that you see and hear and experience.

Scotland is the same. It's not just the country – it's the people, the places, the music, the language, the food and so much more. Scots are known the world over as welcoming, chatty folk who love a good party. If there's a ceilidh (rhymes with "daily") in town, we'll be there! If you don't know, a ceilidh is a loud, lively gathering filled with Scottish music and dances.

Highlanders are renowned for their hospitality, Glaswegians are known for their sense of humour and Edinburgers (that's not a food, by the way) are respected for their culture. Every part of Scotland has its own character.

Scots can also be a bit sentimental at times. We get a tear in our eye when we think of mist-covered mountains, and the sound of bagpipes will have us stomping and "yeeeooch"-ing in no time. People around the world who have Scottish ancestry can be even more passionate about the "old country". The Scottish diaspora (that means people who are Scottish or of Scottish descent who live outside Scotland) numbers in the many millions. In the United States alone, there are more people who claim Scottish ancestry that there are people in Scotland! It seems everyone wants to be Scottish – which is no surprise, because we're great!

GREAT INVENTORS

For such a small country, Scotland has had a huge impact on the world, with some of the most important inventions, discoveries and developments in modern history.

Do you like watching TV (or anything else that has a screen)? Thank you, Scotland!

Got a phone? That's right – it's a Scottish thing.

And there's so much more.

There's **Alan MacMasters**, who invented the first electric toaster and the electric kettle. Born in Edinburgh, he developed the toaster in 1893. The story goes that he was working on lighting for the London Underground when he realized that his bread was being toasted by the heat of some electrical elements lying nearby. Eureka!

Fancy some cold juice from the fridge? Well, say a little thank you to **William Cullen** as you take a sip. He was a Scottish scientist who came up with the first form of artificial refrigeration in the 1740s, by showing how the heating of liquid to a gas can result in cooling. He never actually made a fridge, but he inspired others to put his ideas into practice.

When we say **Williamina Fleming** from Dundee was a star, we mean it in more ways than one. Born in 1857, she later emigrated to America and became a maid to Edward Pickering, director of Harvard College Observatory. She went on to become a member of the observatory staff and was the first woman to hold a formal appointment at Harvard – a very famous American university. During her life, she came up with a way to classify stars based on brightness and size and discovered nearly 400 stars and other objects in space. She classified 10,351 stars and discovered ten novae and fifty-two nebulae. She was out of this world!

We can't end without a shout-out to the big cheeses of Scottish inventing. **John Logie Baird** demonstrated the first working television system in 1926, **Alexander Graham Bell** was granted the first patent for the telephone in 1876 and **Sir Alexander Fleming** discovered penicillin, which marked the start of modern antibiotics and has saved countless millions of lives.

MUSIC

Whether it's the wheeze of an accordion, the jig of a fiddle, the crash of a rock guitar or the thud of a drum, Scots are big on music. Maybe it's all the dreich (rainy) weather and midges, but we love a good tune to cheer us up. It might be traditionally Scottish or bang up to date, but it's usually accompanied by a good dance.

You can often hear folk music being played in pubs and at wild **ceilidhs**, where Scottish country dancing takes on a life of its own. It's usually a miracle that there are no serious injuries suffered during a **Dashing White Sergeant** or an **Eightsome Reel**. The classic instruments for a ceilidh or folk band would be accordion, fiddle, drums and guitar, with optional pipes or whistle.

One of Scotland's oldest folk instruments is the **clàrsach**, a harp with a curved top and side.

And of course, we can't mention Scottish musical instruments without talking about **bagpipes**. While most people immediately associate them with Scotland, the origins of bagpipes go back thousands of years to far off lands, with some saying they came from India or the Persian Gulf and others North Africa.

The Romans are thought to have brought the bagpipes to Britain nearly 2,000 years ago, and back then they were often made from the skin of a sheep. Maybe that's why they're called BAAA-gpipes!

One of the most popular celebrations of Gaelic music, song and culture is the **Royal National Mòd**, which has been held most years in October since 1892. But, of course, there's more to the Scottish music scene than just traditional music. Many of today's global stars, such as KT Tunstall, Paolo Nutini, Emeli Sandé, Calvin Harris, the Proclaimers, Annie Lennox and Lewis Capaldi, all come from Scotland.

FOOD AND DRINK

Scotland's national animal is the unicorn, our national plant is the thistle and our national motto is "GET IN MA BELLY!" That last one might not be true, but it should be. Scots love their food.

While Scotland might not be renowned for its refined cuisine in the same way countries like France and Italy are, there's still lots to shout about on the food front, from beautiful **seafood** to prime Aberdeen Angus beef to **Scottish salmon** and much more. But ask anyone from around the world to name a Scottish food, and they'll say one thing – **haggis**.

Originally any animal may have been used, as hunters would cook offal, which went off quickly, in the stomach bag. Some people have even suggested haggis originated in England! It's traditionally made from bits of a sheep – finely chopped liver, heart and lungs – mixed with oatmeal, suet, herbs, spices and seasoning, all squeezed into some sheep intestines and boiled or baked. What do you mean you don't want any? It's delicious!

Actually, it really is! No matter how weird it might sound to you, it tastes great with the traditional accompaniment of neeps (turnip or swede) and tatties (potatoes).

Scotland's national drink must be **IRN-BRU**. The advertising slogan for this rust-coloured fizzy juice used to be "Made in Scotland from girders" (girders are the huge metal beams used to help build bridges and the like), but we've checked the ingredients and it definitely isn't, so slurp away!

You can't forget the Scottish classic that is **Cullen skink**, which sounds more like a character from Harry Potter than a dish. It's a creamy soup made from smoked haddock, potato and leek and is guaranteed to give you a warm fishy hug on a cold Scottish winter day. It comes from the village of Cullen in Moray and every year the Cullen Skink World Championships are held there to find the best Cullen skink chef on the planet.

Porridge is another traditional Scottish staple that everyone knows – but have you ever heard of a **porridge drawer**? It's said that, in the past, some Scottish homes lined the bottom drawer in a chest of drawers with a tray that porridge could be poured into at night. It would then set firm by morning and could be sliced and wrapped up for a lovely lunch of cold wobbly porridge. Yum! The drawer above warmed up when the porridge was poured in, so babies would be laid in it to sleep and keep cosy.

Finally, if staying healthy isn't a priority, you could a try a Scottish "delicacy" – the **deep-fried Mars bar**! Yes, it really exists. It's a Mars bar covered in batter then deep fried in a chip shop. It was invented at a Scottish chippy in 1995 and you should definitely NOT have one for breakfast every morning.

COMIC BOOK LEGENDS

Scotland has been making kids across the UK giggle for decades. At the heart of all the chuckles is the city of Dundee, which is home to some of Britain's favourite comic characters of all time. The publishing company **DC Thomson** is behind these comic book heroes.

Probably the best-known of all their comics is the **Beano**. It first came out way back in 1938 and is officially the world's longest-running weekly comic. It probably made your great-great-granny and granddad guffaw when they were your age. Beano is where you'll find much-loved characters like the Bash Street Kids, Minnie the Minx and, most famous of all, **Dennis the Menace** and his dog Gnasher – although those two didn't appear until issue number 452. If you come across a copy of the first Beano, don't use it to blow your nose. There are only thought to be twenty left in the whole world and it could be worth up to £20,000, which is no laughing matter! Its sister comic, The Dandy, started even earlier, in 1937, although the last print edition came out in 2012. They still release annuals and summer specials though, so we can still enjoy the adventures of Desperate Dan, Korky the Cat and Bananaman.

Two truly Scottish comic strips and annuals are also printed by DC Thomson – Oor Wullie and The Broons. If you're English that translates as Our William and The Browns!

The Broons features a big Scottish family who live in a flat at 10 Glebe Street in the fictional Scottish town of Auchentogle. There's Maw, Paw, Maggie, Daphne, Joe, Hen, Horace, the Twins and the Bairn. Granpaw Broon also appears regularly and is always getting up to mischief.

100

If you ever get your hands on a 1964 Broons annual, look out for a mystery. In one strip there are THREE twins (triplets!). To this day no one knows if it was a mistake by legendary illustrator Dudley D. Watkins or an intentional little joke.

Oor Wullie was also co-created and drawn by Dudley. This cheeky Scottish lad is probably best known for wearing dungarees and sitting on a metal bucket. A 2004 survey voted Wullie "Scotland's Favourite Son", beating William Wallace, film star Sir Sean Connery and poet Robert Burns!

FAMOUS SCOTS

Who's the most famous living Scot? Oor Wullie might be top dog in Scotland itself, but around the world some real-life Scottish people (sorry, Wullie) are big names. From the big screen to TV, sport to comedy, Scots have risen to the top on the global stage.

One of Scotland's best-loved stars is comedian **Billy Connolly**. With his trademark beard and big hair, he's made people laugh their socks off in countries far and wide. His nickname is "The Big Yin" (The Big One) and he was known for wearing a pair of huge yellow boots in the shape of bananas on stage back in the 1970s.

When it comes to sport, few can top the achievements of tennis star **Sir Andy Murray**, who has won three Grand Slam titles and two men's singles Olympic gold medals. In 2013, he became the first British winner of the men's singles title at Wimbledon since Fred Perry seventy-seven years earlier. Fun fact – his middle name is Barron!

Sir Chris Hoy is another sporting legend. He was one of the best cyclists the world has ever seen. With a total of seven Olympic medals, six gold and one silver, Hoy is the second most successful Olympic cyclist of all time. After retiring from cycling, he decided to go a bit faster – by becoming a racing car driver!

Rowing superstar **Dame Katherine Grainger** from Bearsden is Britain's most decorated female Olympian ever – an amazing achievement. Not a bad person to have in your rowing boat at the local boating pond...

What about the movies? Scots seem to be big when it comes to sci-fi and fantasy. Just look at Ewan McGregor, who played Obi-Wan Kenobi in the **Star Wars** franchise. His uncle, Denis Lawson, played starfighter pilot Wedge Antilles in two of the original Stars Wars movies and one of the recent ones.

Inverness-born Karen Gillan first became famous as Amy Pond, **Doctor Who**'s companion. Then she hit Hollywood, playing Nebula in Marvel's *Guardians of the Galaxy Vol. 1* and *Vol. 2* and *Avengers: Infinity War*. It might be hard to recognize her, though – her character is covered from head to toe in bright blue make-up!

Speaking of Doctor Who, Ncuti Gatwa, who was announced as the fourteenth Doc in 2022, is the first Black actor to play the role. He moved to Scotland as a toddler when his family fled from war in Rwanda, and was homeless at one point before he got his big break in acting.

One of the most famous authors ever, JK Rowling, wrote her early **Harry Potter** books in Edinburgh, where she lived at the time. They were turned into one of the biggest fantasy movie series ever. Scottish actor Robbie Coltrane starred as Hagrid and was actually the first actor to be cast in the movies. During filming, an animatronic head with moving eyes and lips, based on a mould of Robbie's face, was worn by stunt doubles during Hagrid's action scenes.

The actor Katie Leung is also a Scottish Harry Potter star. She was born in Dundee and went on to appear in the films as Cho Chang after her dad spotted an advertisement for a role in *Harry Potter and the Goblet of Fire* in 2005. She must have been good, because she beat more than 3,000 other girls for the part!

102

WOULD YOU BELIEVE IT?

Victoria Drummond, born in Perthshire in 1894, was Queen Victoria's goddaughter. She could have led a life of privilege, but instead became Britain's first female marine engineer. She was a hero, too. During the Second World War, she was awarded an MBE for bravery after single-handedly keeping the engines of the SS *Bonita* running while it was being bombed by German planes.

The People newspaper (28 September 1941) reported: "The danger was tremendous. She ordered the engine-room staff on deck … In that inferno of steam gone mad, she stayed alone. She held back the escaping steam. With her two hands, she maintained the power of the ship, absolutely alone. You must make a picture of that in your mind – of this indomitable woman holding down something like the force of a volcano while bomb after bomb exploded above her."

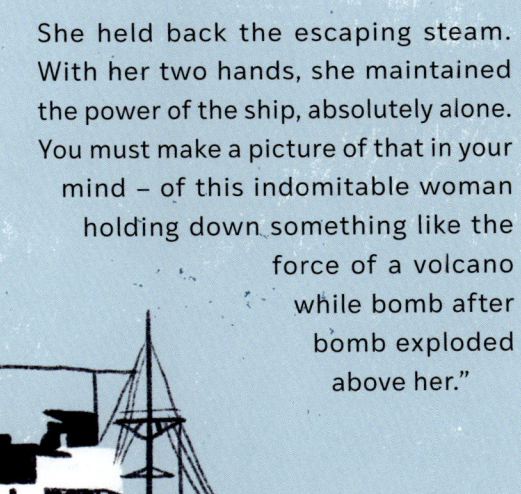

Hogmanay is probably Scotland's most famous tradition. It's celebrated on 31 December into 1 January – New Year's Eve. It's not certain where the word comes from, but some experts claim it has a French root, from the word *hoguinané*, which means a gift given at New Year. "First footing" after midnight on Hogmanay is still popular – a dark-haired man should be the first to visit a home, carrying shortbread, coal and whisky, ensuring good luck for the household. It's said a dark male was considered good because a visit from a blond Viking wasn't particularly lucky, back in the day.

Shinty is a rough and furiously fast game played mainly in the Highlands of Scotland. Imagine hockey but much wilder! The shinty stick is called a caman and players can tackle each other using their bodies as long as it's shoulder-to-shoulder. The game has similarities to the Irish sport of hurling and rules have been devised that combine shinty and hurling so Scotland and Ireland can play annual international matches.

Scotland is known as the birthplace of **golf**. It dates back to the 15th century and was so popular it was even banned in 1457 as it was seen as a distraction from military training! The world's oldest existing golf course is Musselburgh Old Links, which was first documented in 1672. Though it's said that Mary, Queen of Scots herself had a wee putt there even earlier, in 1567.

The wonderfully named tradition of **Whuppity Scoorie** dates back to the early nineteenth century in the town of Lanark. On 1 March the arrival of spring is celebrated by children running clockwise around St Nicholas Kirk, whooping and swinging paper balls on strings above their heads as they run. After three laps, they have a scramble (scrabbling about wildly for coins thrown for them). Sounds quite bonkers – but fun! Perhaps they should introduce Whuppity Scoorie to the Olympics...

Stan Laurel, one half of silent comedy legends Laurel and Hardy, grew up in Glasgow. His dad was the manager of the city's Metropole Theatre, and young Stan began his working life there. His stage debut was at Glasgow's Panopticon Music Hall when he was just sixteen years old. The theatre still exists, located above an amusement arcade in the city, and is said to be the oldest surviving music hall in the world.

ABOUT THE CONTRIBUTORS

The author

CHAE STRATHIE

Chae is an award-winning children's author and magazine editor based in Dundee, who grew up in New Lanark, a tiny village surrounded by a forest in Scotland, which probably explains a lot.

His first attempt at professional writing was creating a Star Wars comic at the age of seven. He sold two copies and made a total of four pence.

A regular at major book festivals, Chae has toured the length and breadth of the UK and visited schools as far afield as Romania, reading his stories, acting the goat and singing silly songs about worm ice cream, Hercules and beard-growing.

The artists

HAZEL DUNN

Hazel is a Glasgow-based designer who works between illustration, textiles, printmaking and community-engaged arts projects. Her style is influenced by the Bauhaus, the Russian avant-garde and Folk Art movements, with wider inspiration drawn from themes of childhood, print process and the natural world.

JILL CALDER

Jill is an award-winning illustrator and calligrapher based in Fife. She loves drawing, ideas, colour, ink, typography, stories, books, dogs and deadlines. Jill blends traditional and digital image-making methods as seamlessly as possible resulting in whimsical illustrations with broad appeal. As a result, her work is commissioned for children's picture books, huge hospital murals, financial and scientific reports, branding Scotch beer and whisky and global advertising campaigns.

CATRIONA PHILLIPS

Catriona is an artist and illustrator from the Isle of Skye, currently based in Perthshire, Scotland. She specializes in ink and watercolour illustrations and particularly enjoys drawing beautiful old buildings, fancy flowers and gardens, and all kinds of tasty food.

HELEN KELLOCK

Helen is an award-winning illustrator and writer based in Glasgow. She graduated from Glasgow School of Art in 2018 with a Distinction in her Illustration Masters and has since won The Batsford Prize 2018, Children's Illustration, and been highly commended for both The Macmillan Book Prize 2018 and The Adobe Design Achievement Awards 2018. At the heart of Helen's practice is a love of drawing narrative, and making picture books.

LAUREN MORSLEY

Lauren is an illustrator and printmaker based in Fife. She specialises in bold and colourful designs which create other worlds to explore. Her work is often inspired by intriguing stories, places, and people. Alongside her commission work for various clients, she makes and sells her own prints and products, full of wiggly armed and long legged characters.

KATIE SMITH

Katie is an illustrator based in Glasgow, currently studying Communication Design at Glasgow School of Art. Her work is playful and colourful, inspired by all the good things in life – nature, female beauty, plants and sunshine. She uses bright colours to promote a positive attitude and wellbeing to brighten up your day. Her illustrations are created using a mix of both analogue and digital techniques.

INDEX

Antonine Wall **22**

bagpipes **13, 97**
basking sharks **44–45**
Battle of Bannockburn **54**
Battle of the Clans **52**
Battle of Culloden **50, 58**
Battle of Dun Nechtain **25, 26**
Battle of Falkirk **54**
Battle of Gruinart **60**
Battle of Killiecrankie **69**
Battle of Largs **53**
Battle of Mons Graupius **57**
Battle of Pinkie **58**
Battle of the Shirts **59**
Battle of the Spoiling Dyke **52**
Battle of Stirling Bridge **54**
beavers **40**
Ben Nevis **19, 27**
Blue Men of the Minch **89**
Burke and Hare **45**

Caledonia **22, 28**
Caledonian Orogeny **19–20**
castles **50, 55–57, 59, 61, 68, 71**

ceilidhs **94, 97**
Central Belt **34**
cities **34**
clans **51–52, 59, 66, 74–75**
comic books and strips **100–101**
Connolly, Billy **101**
Crathes Castle **68**
Cullen skink **99**
culture **92–105**

Discovery, RSS **37**
Doggerland **28**
Doric **28**
dragons **86–87**
Drummond, Victoria **103**
Dundee **17, 37, 86–87**
Dunnottar Castle **57**

Edinburgh **16, 34, 35–36, 45, 69–70, 88, 94**
Edinburgh Castle **35, 55–56, 59, 61, 71**
Eilean Donan Castle **57**
England and the English **50, 54, 56, 58**
Eriskay **43**

fairy folk **60, 80, 81–82**
Fairy Pools and Fairy Glen **80**
famous Scots **101–104, 105**
festivals **35, 98**
First and Second World Wars **44, 59, 61, 103–104**
Firth of Forth **25, 43**
Flannan Isles **89**
flora and fauna **40–42**
food and drink **98–100**

Forest of Rothiemurchus **75**
Forth Bridge **36–37, 44**

Gaelic **23–24, 39**
geology **18, 19–20**
ghosts **64–75**
Glasgow **17, 34, 35, 36, 73, 88, 94, 105**
Glencoe massacre **74–75**
Glenfinnan Viaduct **37**
Glenmore Forest Park **80**
golf **105**

Hadrian's Wall **22, 27**
haggis **12, 98**
Harry Potter films **37, 102**
Highland Clearances **23**
Highlands **17, 20**
history **18–29**
see also warfare
Hogmanay **104**
House of Dun **66–67**
Hoy, Sir Chris **101**

Inchgarvie Island **44**
Inner Hebrides **39**
inventors **95–96**
IRN-BRU **99**
islands **39–40, 43–44**
Islay **39**

Jacobite rising **58**
James VI and I **56, 58, 83**

Jura **39**
Kelpies (sculpture) **37**
kelpies (water spirits) **82–83, 89**
languages **23–24, 28, 39**

Laurel, Stan **105**
legends **38, 40, 42, 60, 66, 78–89**
see also ghosts
Lewis and Harris **18, 39**
Lewisian gneisses **18**
Loch Morar **38**
Loch Ness **38**
Loch Ness monster **85–86**
lochs **38–39**

Maeshowe **21**
Mars bars, deep-fried **100**
Mary King's Close, Edinburgh **69–70**
Mons Meg **61**
mountains **19, 27**
Murray, Sir Andy **101**
music **97–98**

Neolithic period **21**
New Lanark **44**

111

Orkney **17, 21, 53, 84, 87**
Outer Hebrides **18, 23, 39**

Palace of Holyroodhouse **36**
Picts **25–26, 57**
pine martens **41**
plague **69–70**
Politician, SS **43**
population **16, 17, 34**
porridge **99**
prehistoric Scotland **18, 20–21**
regions **16**

River Tay **37, 44, 72**
Robert the Bruce **54, 55, 56, 68**
Rockall **40**
Romans **22, 25, 27, 28, 57, 97**
Rosemary Bank **27**
Rosslyn Chapel **74**

Scotland Street School, Glasgow **73**
Scotland's Secret Bunker **43**
Scots language **24, 28**
Scottish diaspora **94**
Scottish Parliament **35–36**
selkies **84–85**
Shetland **42, 53, 84, 87**
shinty **104**

shipbuilding **36**
Skara Brae **21**
Skye **39, 52, 80**
Southern Uplands **20**
Stirling Castle **56**
Stoor Worm **87**
superstitions **66, 72**

Tantallon Castle **57, 61**
Tay Bridge disaster **72**
thistles **41–42**
timelines **29, 60–61**
Traprain Law **27**

unicorn **88**
Union of the Crowns **58**

Vikings **53, 57**
volcanic activity **27**

Wallace, William **54**
warfare **26, 44, 48–61, 69, 103–104**
weather **42**
Whuppity Scoorie **105**
wildcats **41**
wildlife **40–41, 44–45**
witches **83–84**
wolves **40**

112